SOULS OF THE SEA

WITHDRAWN

SOULS OF THE SEA

DAMIEN TIERNAN

HODDER
HEADLINE
IRELAND

Copyright © 2007 Damien Tiernan

First published in 2007 by Hodder Headline Ireland

1

The right of Damien Tiernan to be identified as the Author of the Work has been asserted by him in accordance with the Copyright, Designs and Patents Act, 1988.

A CIP catalogue record for this title is available from the British Library.

ISBN 978-0-340-95251-1

Typeset in Sabon by Hodder Headline Ireland
Cover design by Anú design, Tara
Printed and bound in Great Britain by Clays, St Ives plc

Hodder Headline Ireland's policy is to use papers that are natural, renewable and recyclable products and made from wood grown in sustainable forests. The logging and manufacturing processes are expected to conform to the environmental regulations of the country of origin.

Hodder Headline Ireland
8 Castlecourt Centre
Castleknock
Dublin 15
Ireland

A division of Hachette Livre, 338 Euston Road, London NW1 3BH, England

CONTENTS

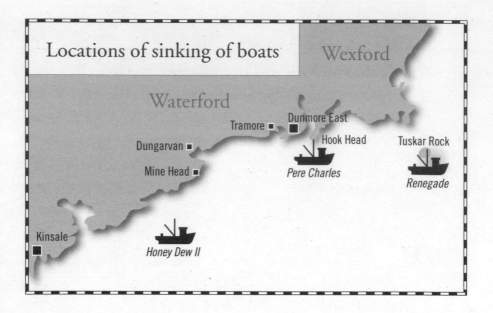

Locations of sinking of boats

Wexford

Waterford

Tramore ■　Dunmore East ■

Dungarvan ■　　　　　　Hook Head　　Tuskar Rock

Mine Head ■　　　　　　Pere Charles　　Renegade

Kinsale ■

Honey Dew II

This book is dedicated to fishermen and women
and their families.

Prologue

'She's broached on me. Stand by us.'

Those were the last words spoken to the outside world by Tom Hennessy, skipper of the *Pere Charles*, a large fishing trawler that sank off the coast of Wexford on 10 January 2007. The loss of the *Pere Charles*, only 2 miles from land, signalled the start of a spate of sinkings that left the fishing communities of Dunmore East, Kilmore Quay and Kinsale reeling in shock. For those who make their living from the sea, they know they are risking life and limb every time they head out into open water, but they live in hope that they will return safely, like the last time and the time before that. Hours after the *Pere Charles* sank, the *Honey Dew II* went to its watery grave less than 20 miles away in a ferocious storm. Just six days later, a third boat sank.

In that stormy week in January, seven men did not return safely – they will never return.

This is the story of the *Pere Charles* and the *Honey Dew II*, of their skippers, Tom Hennessy and Ger Bohan, and of the men who crewed them and went down with them. It is an account of the horror the sea can hold for those who fish its waters – imagine being far from shore, with the wind screeching, the waves rising, the rain pelting incessantly, imagine the darkness of a vast, empty sea engulfed in a raging storm: how do you survive?

This is also the story of the fishing industry in modern Ireland, whose work takes place in one of the most dangerous workplaces it's possible to find. These stories have to be told because the memories of those who have been lost demands that we stand by them. We can do that by learning from their deaths, by recognising the economic pressures that threaten to swamp fishermen and wreck their livelihoods and by calling for a review of the policies and practices that have led to a situation where seven men going about their daily jobs can be killed within hours of each other.

This, then, is a story of fear and horror, of death and survival, of loss and heartbreak, of remembering and regretting. But it is also an asking why: why did these sturdy trawlers sink? Why wasn't the loss of the *Honey Dew II* realised immediately by those monitoring Irish territorial waters? Why do fishermen take to sea during stormy weather? Why do we continue to accept death as part of the lot of our fishermen? These questions have been ignored for too long.

PART I

FISHING IN THE CELTIC SEA

1

The *Pere Charles* and Her Skipper

Dunmore East is full of Powers. So many, in fact, that nicknames are needed: 'Butler' Power, the 'Bulligan' Power, 'Billys' Power, 'Dee' Power, 'Dollys' Power, 'Copper' Power, 'Johns' Power, 'Robin' Power, 'Terrance' Power, 'Fancy' Power, 'The Vet' Power, 'Joss' Power, 'Vesty' Power, 'Showery' Power, 'Tenant' Power, Ritchie 'Cu' Power, Ritchie 'Waxy' Power, Paddy 'Sos' Power, 'Spanners' Power, 'Maurice the Crab' Power, the 'Rocky' Power, and the 'Phantom' Power – to name but a few.

As some of the locals say, 'there's a ball of Powers' and there are not enough nicknames to go around. Being a postman in Dunmore is a difficult job. Those who run the pub up on the main street are known as 'the Butcher Powers', and the pub is known as 'The Butchers'. It was here that Lulu Doyle first met Tom

Hennessy, back in 1999, when she was twenty years old and he just twenty-two. From the moment she first saw him standing there – tall, dark-haired with deep brown eyes – she was smitten. Tom's uncle Pat introduced the two of them. Tom was instantly attracted to Lulu, and it wasn't long before they were going out together.

That first night, Tom told her that he fished in Kerry on small boats and up along the Clare coast, that he had done an Engineering course in Carlow Institute of Technology for two years and that he had only come to Dunmore 'for a week', but had decided to stay. He was living up the hill in a rented house with his uncles, Pat and John, and fishing with Richard Power on the *Stella Mar*.

At the end of 1999 Tom and Lulu head to the Magharees, in Kerry, to ring in the millennium. They go to Tom's family home. It's a four-hour drive from Dunmore East to this small, narrow, postcard-perfect peninsula of land jutting out into Tralee Bay. Surrounded by water on three sides, visitors sometimes feel they are entering a time-warp: 'you might come here for a day, but you mightn't get out for a week'. The scattered houses hunker down away from the near-constant wind as it skims in off the Atlantic. Everyone is friendly and Tom's family warm to Lulu immediately. She hears him called Tomaisín for the first time, which is how he is known in Kerry – 'young Tomas'.

Some months later Tom and Lulu rent a house together in Dunmore and within eighteen months are engaged, but wedding plans are put on hold for a while because Lulu is pregnant. Their daughter Christine is born, followed a year later by Jane, as beautiful as her sister.

Tom is a skipper now and fishing a lot on the *Boy Conor*, with his uncle Pat in tow, a man with whom he loves to fish because he's so dependable and hard-working. In 2005 a new boat arrives into Dunmore. It's considered one of the best to come to the south-east in years. It's called the *Pere Charles* and Tom Hennessy is going to be its skipper. Tom can't stop talking about it and at the first opportunity brings Lulu down to have a look. It's a steel boat with a shelter deck, which means the only area where water can enter the boat is from its stern, at the back. The front and sides are 'sheltered' and protected by steel sheeting. The *Pere Charles* is 19.81m long, 6.5m wide and has a draught of 3.1m. It's powered by a Mitsubishi 600hp main engine, with a 30hp generator providing back-up. Tom shows Lulu all around inside the wheelhouse, with its fancy computer screens and gadgets. She's delighted that he is so excited about this new venture.

Tom loved the *Pere Charles* from the first time he saw it a few months earlier, when he and boat-owner Michael Walsh had driven to Skerries in north County Dublin to see it. The two men knew this was the boat for them. They got the price down from €400,000 to €380,000. Michael Walsh knew it was a lot of money and would mean massive bank loans, but this was the boat he really wanted, and he knows boats.

Sometimes known as 'Mickey Winch' or 'Mickey the Winch' (at the age of eight he tried to tell older boys how to work a particular winch on a boat, hence the nickname), Michael Walsh has been fishing all his life and he has great respect for Tom Hennessy. Michael is very well-known in fishing communities, particularly as he helped to set up the South and East Fishermen's Organisation. His plan is that the *Pere Charles* will be used to catch whitefish and prawns over the summer months and herring during some of the winter months.

On the *Pere Charles* the main hatch is at the stern, not up front as in most French trawlers. The time Michael was buying the boat, he was attending an EU Regional Advisory Council meeting in Dublin, at which there were representatives of many European fishing nations. He decided to ask one of the French men, through an interpreter, if he knew of a boat called the *Pere Charles*. Without hesitation, the man confirmed he knew the boat and said it had been built for herring and mackerel fishing, and that its previous owners had used it for this (and for prawns and whitefish). Michael couldn't believe it – this boat was perfect for him.

The *Pere Charles* was built in Etaples-sur-Mer in France in 1982, but since 2001 had been working out of Skerries under the ownership of Noel Wilde. When Michael and Tom bring the boat to Dunmore, Johnny Clooney from Passage East carries out some re-wiring and installs a new CCTV system, giving the skipper full coverage of events on the stern, on the deck and in the engine room. All the safety requirements are met, including checks on the EPIRB.[1] The trawler is seen as a great addition to the fleet in Dunmore. Fishermen tell their friends about it and on Sunday evenings some take their wives or children for a drive down to the quay, just to look at it.

Tom is delighted with the boat. He enjoys acquainting himself with all the electronics and engineering aspects, and feels he can

---

[1] An EPIRB is an Emergency Position Indicating Radio Beacon. Small and light enough to be held in one hand, it transmits a one-way distress signal that is activated either manually or automatically. If a boat sinks, an EPIRB fitted with a hydrostatic release unit will float free and automatically transmit a distress signal, which relays the vessel's exact position to the nearest Coast Guard co-ordination centre.

sort out any problem that may arise. He is very much a fisherman at heart, a passion many 'landlubbers' find hard to comprehend. When he's not fishing, he's talking about fishing, which is why he spends so much time with his brother, Pat Frank, because they are both happy to talk fishing for hours on end. Tom also reads lots of books about fishing and the sea. He can relate to those stories. He loves to read about people who have had to endure hardship, especially hardship at sea. One of his heroes is Tom Crean, the Kerryman who became a famed Antarctic explorer. When Tom read a book about Crean some time ago, he talked with Pat Frank about how men like Tom Crean had to face death. He's not one for philosophical musings on life and death, but he tells Pat Frank how he was struck by Crean's fortitude and determination at every step on his arduous journeys and his battles with death.

Pat Frank no longer fishes himself and when they were fishing, he and Tom never dwelled on the idea of death. The way they see it, there are enough old men in pubs and on quays around the coast to testify to the fact that the sea doesn't take everyone.

When he's at home, Tom watches documentaries and cowboy films. His favourite is *The Big Country*, in which Gregory Peck's character is a retired sea-captain come out west to marry his girl. In one sequence he uses a compass to navigate across the wide-open prairies, which to him are just like the wide-open seas. It doesn't matter to Tom that the 'Hennessys' in the film are really called the 'Hannasseys' (they sound the same), he just loves the line when Charlton Heston warns Peck's intended: 'The reason I mention it is that the Hannessy boys are in town. They've been drinking.'

In the past, Pat Frank and Tom did some drinking. They've always been best buddies. Pat Frank is just eleven months older than his brother and when they were children, together they dreamed of a life at sea. Their two uncles, Pat and Mick, were fishermen, so it was in the family. When he was sixteen, Pat Frank rang his uncle Pat, who was fishing from Dunmore East, and asked if he could spend the summer with him. Pat said of course, he'd love to have him with him. So Pat Frank went fishing and loved it.

After he finished his Leaving Cert., Pat Frank didn't bother going to college, but went fishing straight away. He headed to the Bay of Biscay, hunting for tuna. Tom would have liked that, too, but their mother, Julia, thought further education might serve him better, so he went to college in Carlow. He stuck it for two years, but left and went to the fishermen in Kerry, looking for work. After the Bay of Biscay, Pat Frank spent a few years fishing off the coast of Kerry and Clare. But bad winter weather off the west coast seriously limits days at sea, so he decided to head to Dunmore East, where he quickly established himself. The weeks became months and before he knew it, Pat Frank hadn't been home for two years. Dunmore had got under his skin. Then Tom joined him, and the real fun began.

They shared a house and when they weren't fishing enjoyed a mad social life. They loved every minute of life in Dunmore, on the quay, on the waves. Some might say they were out of touch with the real world, but this was their reality. All they talked about was fishing, girls, fishing, horses, fishing and girls. They had plenty of money and not enough weekends in which to spend it. They didn't care about the world outside Dunmore. It's like that in some, although not all, coastal villages. That's why the phrase 'fishing community' can mean just that: a commune, an enclosed order, a family. 'It was mayhem,' says Pat Frank, who was twenty-four at the time; his brother twenty-three. 'It was like who could be the toughest, it was pure macho shit. There was one time a fellow who used to be in the Foreign Legion got a job with us; we wrecked him; we were hauling every few hours for ten days; mental stuff; he couldn't keep up with us; so we reckoned that we were tougher than the Foreign Legion. Then two massive fellows from the Russian Army came to work on the boat, and they were doing chin-ups off one hand and we were looking at them saying, "We'll sort them fuckers out". On the fourth morning, the Russians couldn't get out of bed they were so tired and wrecked.'

So Tom and Pat reckoned they were tougher than the lads in the Russian Army.

'And then we worked with a lad who was just out of jail for murder, and we fucked him up as well. We reckoned we were the toughest lads in the world.'

Tom loved the book *The Perfect Storm*, but never thought much of the film. Some time after he read it, his brother Pat Frank was in America, fishing out of Gloucester, the same port from which the *Andrea Gail* fished – the boat at the centre of the book – and the same area that was hit by that massive storm back in 1991. One of the men who died on the *Andrea Gail* was Bobby Shatford. When Pat Frank fished out of Gloucester, he was in the same crew as Bobby's brother, who has the nickname *the Shadow*. Tom would ring from Ireland for a chat with Pat Frank about the fishing off the Grand Banks, east of Gloucester. Putting on his best American accent, Tom loved repeating a line from the film: 'The Grand Banks is no place to be in Okk-toe-burrr.'

When they fished together, the Hennessy boys went out in all sorts of weather, but most importantly of all, they had great freedom. For any fisherman, freedom is the stuff of which dreams are made.

It was in those years that they met Michael Walsh. Eventually Pat Frank went back to Kerry to start his own landscaping business, but Tom stayed in Dunmore, stayed with Michael Walsh and the life he loved so much.

For Michael, as for every boat-owner, fishing is all about turnover. If you don't turn over the money, you can't pay the loan on the boat or pay the crew; if you can't pay the crew, you won't keep the crew. Turnover is based on the gross earnings of a boat per day, and a boat-owner knows the boat has to do X amount of days in a year for him to be able to pay the bills. For example, a boat-owner might reckon his boat has to fish 200 days a year and make €1,200 a day – it needs to gross €240,000 in a year. Now the boat may not take in €1,200 worth of fish every day, but at the end of the year the owner will be expecting the average to work out at that. A boat-owner is under pressure all the time, trying to make the facts and figures tally. A weather forecast never appears on a bank statement.

So far this year, Tom Hennessy and the *Pere Charles* have had a busy time catching prawns and whitefish. However, the bad weather has meant fishing in October, November and now December hasn't been great. Tom fished for herrings a few years ago in another boat, but didn't make a lot of money at it and thinks the ends don't justify the means. But now that the *Pere Charles* has been tied up at the quayside for nearly four weeks, he's thinking about the herrings and the long winter ahead.

Sixth December 2006 is the first time Tom fishes for herrings from the *Pere Charles*. Michael Walsh organises for the small, but necessary, changes to be made to equip the boat for herring fishing: new boards for the pounds in the hold to allow for herrings to be stored, and a different net is fitted.

Tom and his crew fish just off Hook Head, with the *Suzanna G*, in what is called 'pair-fishing'. On that first night they took in 'a good shot of herrings': 28 tonnes. Tom tells Michael Walsh he's surprised at how quickly they killed the fish. The next day they went out again and this time landed 34 tonnes of herrings. Tom was happy with how both trips went. They weren't able to go out again that week and stopped fishing for herrings on the evening of 7 December, knowing they would go back out in January. They decided to go fishing for prawns for whatever days they could for the rest of December. From Michael Walsh's perspective, it is a great achievement to have another pair of Dunmore-based vessels out herring fishing again.

Yes, this could be the start of something great.

2

The *Honey Dew II* and Her Skipper

Ger Bohan's grandfather, James (Jim), came from Aughavaas in Co. Leitrim, hundreds of miles to the north of Kinsale in Co. Cork, where Ger now lives and fishes. The Leitrim Bohans believe the surname originated in France and will tell you that the Bohanes settled in the county in the 1790s. Jim Bohan joined the newly formed Garda Síochána in 1922, just after the Civil War, and was stationed in various towns around the country before finally ending up in Kinsale. In those days, many Leitrim people never saw the sea for as long as they lived because people didn't travel far and the county has only 2.5 miles of coastline. Jim Bohan did live to see the sea, and he fell in love with it and with Kinsale. The name Bohan is well-known in Co. Cork, but locals pronounce it with a strong emphasis on the second syllable: Bo-HAAN. The Leitrim

Bohan is different, it's BO-han, with the emphasis on the first syllable. The lads on the quay in Kinsale joke that their way is right.

At the age of ten Ger Bohan went out on a boat with his uncle and won an angling competition, an event that got him dreaming about a life on the water. He saved money from summer jobs and three years later bought a little rowing boat, and even managed to get an outboard engine for it. Although not fond of school, he studied well and got his Leaving Certificate. 'If I'd known it was that easy, Dad,' he said to his father, Sean, afterwards, 'I'd have gone for the higher grades.'

The only thing Ger ever wanted to be was a fisherman. He went up to Greencastle, in 6. Donegal, to do his skipper's ticket, a course that would allow him to captain a boat officially. Back in Kinsale, he takes Sean out with him one day in a small lobster boat, off to Roche's Point in a big swell. Sean watches as Ger stands up on the rising, just below the top of the boat, and pulls hard on the rope attached to the lobster pots. His sense of balance is perfect. Up from the deep comes a milk crate with the words 'Cork Milk Producers' on its side. Ger has adapted the crates to use them for catching lobster. Sean is amazed not only by his son's ingenuity but by his ability to haul in the pots in rough seas while standing precariously on the edge of the boat. A natural, he thinks to himself.

The sea is Ger's life, his greatest interest. When Sebastian Junger's book *The Perfect Storm* was made into a movie, he couldn't wait to see it, and has re-watched it many times since. Mary, Ger's wife, jokes that the DVD is nearly worn out, it's been played so much. Ger loves heading out in his trawler past the Old Head of Kinsale on a sunny day, imagining he's George Clooney in *The Perfect Storm*. He repeats the words from the film: 'The best feeling in the world.' He wonders if Clooney ever really went out fishing like that. Sometimes when he's out at sea, Ger rings or texts Mary before she goes to bed and tells her to dream that she's sleeping with George tonight, 'but tomorrow, when I'm home, you'll be with a real fisherman'.

To Mary, it seems like only yesterday that she first met Ger. She was working in a restaurant called The Shack and Ger would call in some evenings after fishing because he fancied one of the younger waitresses. At first, Mary had no real interest in him. When they'd look at Ger, she and the other waitresses would joke, 'Sure, what would we do with him if we got him?' The girl Ger was pursuing wasn't interested, so Mary asked him out and they hit it off immediately. One night, in the early days of their romance, Mary was driving Ger home up the old Bandon road out of Kinsale in her creaking Renault. Her house was miles beyond Ger's parents' house, and as they neared his stop she slowed down and said, 'Well, do you want to get off here or will I keep going?' 'Ah sure, keep going,' said the big curly-haired man beside her.

And they've kept going ever since.

Sometimes Ger would come in from fishing at 3.00am and cycle the 6 miles to where Mary was living with her three-year-old son, Anthony. Ger and Mary loved each other's straight-talking, no-nonsense attitude to life. There was no need for years of courting; within a short while Ger moved in with Mary and they were happy with the teenage-like speed of their relationship.

Mary and Ger moved and have been in a rented, semi-detached, two-storey house for nearly twelve years beside Ger's parents, Sean and Anne. The two families share the big back garden and the children love the freedom of running between the two. When Ger comes home from a fishing trip, Mary and the children normally hear him before they see him. He'll slide back the front door and roar that he's home and then roar all through the house until he finds the four children: Anthony (18), Sally Jean (11), James (9) and Joseph (6). They love him to bits. He's mad about them.

Mary doesn't get much done whenever Ger is home because he follows her around the house, talking all the time. And if he wakes at 7.00am, he'll wake her so they can have a chat. The days when he's home are chaotic, special and never boring. When he's not out fishing, he normally goes down to the pier in the morning to do a few jobs on the boat. At around 9.30am he'll ring Mary and they'll either have breakfast at home or in a little restaurant in Kinsale called Cucinas, more often than not with their friends Johnny Walsh and Eamonn O'Neill. Scrambled eggs are Ger's favourite.

When Mary and Ger first got together, he was fishing on a boat called the *Ard Beara* and was home most evenings. One day, he said to her, 'I think I'll go out on me own and buy a boat.'

'Do,' says Mary.

So he did.

That was 1994. He got money from Bord Iascaigh Mhara (the Irish fisheries board) and bought the *Boy Evin*, a 52ft boat that was good to them. Sally Jean and James were born, and then Mary's divorce came through (she was one of the first women in Ireland to get a divorce). In 1999, seven years into their relationship, Ger and Mary got married, a memorable and a wonderful day.

While their home life was good, Ger's working life was not running so smoothly as the financial pressures on fishermen were increasing every year. Even if the weather was good, Ger didn't know if he'd make enough money to survive due to the conditions imposed on him by the EU and by the Irish government.

Fishermen were being forced out of the industry one by one. But Ger was also ambitious and the only alternative to bailing out of fishing was to get a bigger boat. Ger sold the *Boy Evin* and in May 2001, on a fine day when their son, Joseph, was only six months old, he bought the *Honey Dew II*. A wooden boat, it had been built in Baltimore, in west Cork, in 1980 and was previously called the *Sé Óg*. The owner, Brendan O'Driscoll, renamed it the *Honey Dew II* because his father, Donal, previously had a boat called the *Honey Dew I*. Brendan sold the boat to Ger for €150,000. Ger then had to buy what is known as 'tonnage' – the equivalent of a milk quota for farmers. The tonnage cost €360,000, so before he has caught a single fish, Ger has spent half-a-million euro on the *Honey Dew II*. He's under serious financial pressure, but is fiercely ambitious to make this major investment work and every surplus euro he earns goes back into the boat, or is used to repay the interest on the loans. Ger and Mary have spent the last fifteen years growing and maturing together and they know how to make ends meet, somehow; as Ger says to her, 'Sure don't we work mighty together, hon'?'

Mary never worries about Ger going fishing. She thinks if he's ever going to die suddenly, it could be in a car crash – never in a fishing accident. It's only in the last while that she's started thinking about how things are beginning to improve for them, in spite of the financial burden under which they labour: 'The children are great, the boat is good, Ger's health is perfect, the fishing's not good, but we'll get by,' she says.

She trusts deeply Ger's love of the sea and his passion for fishing, which is unbounded. Ger has a great interest in fishing methods around the world and Canadian fishing in particular. When he was young, two very good childhood friends, sisters

Deirdre and Fiona Boyle, emigrated to Canada. Ger was devastated to see them go, but that was Ireland in the 1980s, a time when thousands of families left for a better life abroad. Ger kept in contact with the Boyles, travelling over to see them many summers and subsequently developing a deep interest in the fishing techniques of men in places such as Nova Scotia. Fiona and her daughter came over to Ireland in October 2006 for a week and stayed in Fiona's aunt's house. Ger brought his children over and he and Fiona had a great chat about times past, like when he was known as 'Ger Tah-Dah' because he said 'tah-dah' every time he did something.

They laugh at the funny incidents from their childhood, like when Ger mooned at a well-known businessman in Kinsale for a dare. All the gang ran, but for some reason Fiona was frozen to the spot and was going to be caught. Such was his loyalty, Ger turned around and went back for her. Or that other time when he, Fiona and Deirdre went out in a rowing boat and the tide carried them out further than expected, and Ger rowed and rowed and rowed for over two hours to get them home safely. Fiona remembers that if Ger was ever worried, he never showed it, he just kept it to himself and remained calm. And he could always be trusted to keep a secret. Fiona has never met a man who lives life to the full, who loves fully and is loved fully in return – and never forgets to tell you he loves you.

The morning after his long reminiscences with Fiona, Ger is steaming out of Kinsale to fish. On his left, Summer Cove and the star-shaped Charles Fort; to his right, James Fort, built in 1607 to help guard the narrow harbour entrance; further out, Hake Head, Holeopen Bay East; and up towards Waterford there's Frower Point, the Sovereign Islands, Oysterhaven, Newfoundland Bay and

Flat Head. The sun rises over the Celtic Sea in a blaze of oranges and reds and makes Ger smile. 'Holy God, that's beautiful,' he thinks. It's not yet 7.00am, but he rings the house in which Fiona is staying and makes her get out of bed to come to the phone.

'Gooooood moooorning! I just got you up so you can have a look at the sunrise. Isn't it just beautiful, girl?' he hollers down the line.

Yes, it is beautiful.

For a seaside town with a fishing economy stretching back generations, it's amazing that nobody from the town has died in a boating tragedy since 1898, when a great storm hit the town on 14 October. That night the sea took four people, including David Cramer, who left a widow and eight children; Patrick Owens, who left six children; and Patrick's son, John Owens. A fundraising committee was set up for the relatives of those lost because none of the men 'possessed any means by any nature whatever beyond their earnings as a fisherman'. The Christian name of the fourth victim has not been recorded, but his surname was Bohane.

3

The *Pere Charles* Crew

December 2006 is a bad month in terms of weather, but Pat Coady has worked in weather a lot worse – weather that can kill if you don't judge it right. Pat knows; he's nearly drowned twice. But he reckons it's more than luck that's kept him alive: there's no way the sea is going to take him because there's no way it's going to take three generations of the one family.

Rose Coady, Pat's mother, lives in Newlyn, in Cornwall. Coming up to Christmas she spends a lot of time down on the pier, half-imagining her husband Steve will be there to greet her. She goes again and again to the spot where he fell in, still trying to make sense of her loss.

At 6.00pm on Friday, 13 January 2006, Steve came back into Newlyn after ten days' hard work at sea on the beam trawler the

Marie Claire. He went up with his friend Steve Atmore to see Rose, who was working in The Dolphin pub, and had a few pints there. He went back down to the boat around 10.30pm to get some sleep before the unloading of the catch, which was due to begin at 3.30am. (If a crew member isn't present for the unloading, he may be docked wages and not be invited back on the next trip.) Steve Coady never missed an unloading. Steve Atmore went down fifteen minutes after him and when he saw all the lights off, he presumed Coady had gone up home. He went in to bed, but the boat's alarms went off. The skipper was alerted, who then rang Coady because he was the boat's engineer. He couldn't contact him. The skipper went down to the boat and they turned on all the lights. There, floating in the water, jammed between the boat and the pier, was Steve Coady.

Rose rang their son, Pa (they've always called Pat 'Pa'), back in Dunmore, to tell him that his dad had fallen into the water, hit his head and drowned. Pat was devastated. Pat and Steve weren't the best of friends at the time Steve emigrated to England, but they had kept in touch nevertheless. Pat had even considered going over to Cornwall to fish with his father, but in the end had opted to stay in Dunmore. It took nearly two weeks for the coroner to release Steve's body for burial in his native Co. Wexford. He was put into the same grave in Rathdangan cemetery in which his father is buried. His father, Patrick (Paddy) Coady, died when his small lobster boat, *The Pride of Bantry* sank in June 1985 near the Saltee Islands on the south Wexford coast. His body wasn't found for twenty-nine days.

At Steve's funeral, people kept shaking their heads and saying how sad it was that both men had been taken by the sea, how hard it must be for Rose. Whenever anybody mentioned his father and grandfather dying at sea, Pa would shy away from it, as if he didn't want to talk about it.

After the burial, people drove the short distance to Scaville's Lodge (formally The Legend) in Duncormick, where Steve had once been a regular, and where Pa loves going for a pint. After a while, Pa put his arm around his lifelong friend, John Burrell, with whom he had fished many times. He hadn't spoken to anybody about what had happened, but now he said softly to his friend, 'Eh, Burrell?'

'What's that, Coady?' John replied.

'At least I won't go that way,' said Pa.

The first time Pa nearly drowned was when he was skipper on the *Notre Dame*. The boat started taking in water as they were heading from Kilmore Quay, in Wexford, to fish at 'the Smalls', down off the Cornish coast. He and the three crewmen managed to get into a life-raft and they all got safely ashore. 'SKIPPER SAVES CREW' was the headline in the local paper and the report praised the quick-thinking of Patrick Coady. Pa can't swim, has never bothered to learn because, as he tells his mother, 'if you go down out there, you might as well not be able, it's not much good to you'.

The second time he nearly drowned was the October before his daughter Treasa was born, in 2001. He was fishing out of Dunmore with some men from Wexford. It was a wet and windy and they were fishing for herrings. Coady was on the deck as they hauled in the net in the middle of the night. Without warning, he slipped and went overboard. The weight of his boots dragged him under the water, but he managed to resurface. One of the men grabbed a life-ring and safety rope and threw it out to Coady, who was splashing frantically in the water. No matter how many times they tried, Coady couldn't reach the rope. He shouted and screamed and went underneath for a second time, but through sheer willpower and massive effort managed to lift his head above the water again. The waves were pushing him away from the boat. The men were about to jump in. He was beginning to pass out and was going down for the third, and probably the last, time when the lads threw the life-ring and rope out again and somehow Coady managed to grab it. He was safe. He was lucky. But what did he do the following evening? He went straight back out fishing for herrings.

Rose knows her son Pat has no fear of the water, that he doesn't fear the sea. For the past while, he's been working with a contractor, putting up poles for the ESB, but Rose wonders if he will go back fishing. She knows he loves it, especially herring fishing. She knows he's a hard worker, that he loves the engine room, loves deck work and loves skippering a boat. She knows it's in his blood, like his father before him, and his father before him.

And the Coady name is associated with fishing not just in Ireland but in places such as Newfoundland in Canada, to where many Wexford and Waterford families emigrated 200 years ago to fish for cod. Pat Coady in Wexford wasn't to know it, but in 1995 a fishing tragedy occurred in the Bay of Bulls, Newfoundland and five men were drowned: Giles, Barry, Travers, Goldsworthy. And, the fifth? A man by the name of Pat Cody.

Every year, Pa goes out herring fishing for a few nights, for the love of it more than anything. Now, with Christmas only a few weeks away, there's talk that his work with the contractor may be finishing up. He knows another job will start with a different contractor at the end of January, but in the meantime it's a great chance to go back on the herrings for a while. He rings his mother in Newlyn: 'Any chance of you getting me a berth over there, Ma?' Coady gave up fishing a few years ago to spend more time ashore so he could be home in the evenings with his daughter, Treasa.

Rose never used to fear her men going out to sea, but since her husband's death, she regards the water differently. So she has a ready reply for Pa: 'Stay away from it, son, stay with your digger.'

*

Sevastopol is a city of 400,000 people and is the largest fishing port on the Black Sea. It's expensive for Andrey Dyrin to ring home, so he does so only once a week and tries to keep it short. The reason he rings is Natalya, his wife. He has come to Ireland to work to create a better life for both of them and for their daughter.

Being from Sevastopol, Andrey has always had an interest in the sea, and as he had some training in mechanics and engineering, he fancied working on a boat. He didn't want to work from the port in his home city or on a Ukrainian boat, however, as the wages were bad and normally delayed. So for ten months he worked on cruise-liners on the Mediterranean and dreamed of being a skipper, maybe starting with smaller boats and working his way up. He got some experience of the engine room and was fascinated with the workings of vessels. He was also studying maritime matters in an Institute back in Ukraine and was on course to becoming a captain some day.

In 2005 Andrey heard about the great opportunities in the place they called Ireland. He spent his evenings looking at maps of the country and reading books about a romantic, green land; he fell in love with the idea of the island far away, on the edge of Western

Europe. His friend had already made the long journey there and had secured work, and the stories he told Andrey made him even more convinced that Ireland was the place to make his dreams come true. But Natalya was now pregnant, so they decided to remain in Ukraine for a while. In early 2006, Natalya gave birth to their first child, a beautiful girl whom they named Varvara, after Andrey's grandmother (it's a Latin name translated to Russian and means 'Outsider').

Financially, it was very tough to make ends meet with a baby to look after as well, and they talked again about making the move to Ireland, where the job prospects were much better. Andrey wanted to take Natalya and Varvara with him, but it wasn't possible to raise the money for all three to travel. Instead, Andrey organised a visa for himself and they scraped together enough for his air fare. On 10 March 2006 he kissed his daughter and wife goodbye and left for Ireland, lonely, yet excited about the future. He knew Natalya would be feeling very lonely, too, especially as she had to mind the baby on her own, but they knew it was a temporary measure until he had earned enough to bring them both to join him.

Andrey heard work might be available on some of the fishing boats in Waterford, and made his way there. He was introduced to a local man, who got him work on a boat out of Dunmore. When he rang Natalya, she was worried about him working on fishing trawlers; she wanted him to work elsewhere, away from the sea. But it was the best offer and would allow him to send home cheques every month, which is why he is here in the first place. Andrey now rents a room in a house in Waterford City and never misses a fishing trip.

He rings home every week and texts nearly every day. Natalya sends him photographs of Varvara, photographs he keeps with him all the time. When they talk, Andrey tells Natalya how much he misses them both. He tells her that he loves Ireland and thinks it would be a great place to bring up Varvara. He promises he will go back to see them for the first time in over a year in April 2007 and will organise visas for them to return to Ireland with him, where they will live permanently. Natalya likes the sound of Ireland and can't wait to settle down there with her husband and daughter.

The boat Andrey is working on is the *Pere Charles*. Tom Hennessy is a good man to crew with and whenever he rings him, Andrey is always ready and available for work.

*

Billy O'Connor lives in Dunmore with his wife, Mary. Their children have grown up and moved out and are making their own lives now but they keep in close contact. In the house it's just Billy and Mary – and, of course, Rocky, their small, brown, happy, wiry Cairn terrier who is the apple of Billy's eye.

Mary and Billy go walking together alot, but if Billy is away fishing, Mary takes Rocky instead. When Mary knows Billy is due back from a fishing trip, she'll say to Rocky, 'Where's Daddy?' and Rocky will run straight into the front room, rise up on his hind legs and look out the window until Billy comes walking up the driveway. When Billy gets in the door, it takes a while to calm down Rocky. Once Rocky has settled at their feet, Billy sometimes has a small whiskey while Mary tells him all the news of the day or the week. Billy hasn't gone fishing at all over the summer because he wanted to spend the time with Mary. His leg is hurting him more than usual. He has had a slight limp for the past ten years. He worked around the house, painting and doing odd jobs and pottering in the garden. He has heard on the grapevine that Tom Hennessy might be looking for lads to crew the *Pere Charles* for the herring fishing in January; he'll think about it after Christmas; but he decides that if he does go out, it'll be the last time because of his leg.

Billy was a meticulous student at school – intelligent, bright, and disciplined. He fell in love with the Irish language and all things Gaelic and became a fluent Irish-speaker. He loves Irish music as well and is a good singer, often giving a turn when he and Mary are at house parties. When he was seventeen he left school and got a coveted job in Waterford Crystal, or 'the Glass' as it is known locally. It was there he met Mary. Billy was and is a proper gentleman, and Mary fell for him straight away; after only six months' courting, they were married in the cathedral in Waterford City. They always had a longing to move out of the city and eventually got a house in Dunmore. They paid off the mortgage quickly with Billy's redundancy money from 'the Glass'. Billy went out fishing one day and loved it. Later on, his sons Adrian and Donal tried it, but it wasn't for them.

Mary always worries about Billy when he is out at sea. He has never had any close escapes, thankfully, apart from two years ago when something happened on the boat from which he was fishing and the rescue helicopter was sent out to keep an eye on it as it made its way to port. Mary has never been out fishing with him, has never been out past the harbour wall, but she imagines what it's like out there, and she worries.

If Billy has been out fishing and the weather has been atrocious, he'll come back in and tell her it's been a bad day, but he never makes a big deal about it. In the past he was normally out fishing for up to ten days at a time, but sometimes would spend three weeks out 'on the big ones' near the Isle of Man or the Sherkin Islands. The only consolation at the time was that the children were no longer small. Since he gave up long-haul fishing, Mary has got used to having him around the house and now can't imagine it any other way.

*

Pat Hennessy has been in Dunmore for nearly twenty years now and he loves living there. He is a good-looking man with a full head of hair and a charming smile. He can eat like the proverbial horse, but never puts on weight. Pat now lives in an apartment near the fire station in Dunmore, just above the take-away.

Pat (48) is the youngest of seven siblings and his mother died when he was only two years old, so his sister Josie helped rear him. Pat has always been very close to his brother, Tom Apple (Tomaisín's father) and later on Julia, his sister-in-law. Pat has worked all over the country – on roadworks in Newtown-mountkennedy in Co. Wicklow; as a farm manager near Castlegregory; and fishing out of Dingle, Fenit and Dunmore East. His great-grandfather lived until he was 106 (he collapsed while tarring the roof of a cottage) and his grandfather, who lived to the age of eighty-six, was a fisherman. So it's in the Hennessys' blood. Pat has fished with every skipper in Dunmore and loves being out with his nephew, Tomaisín, or their friend, Gerry Moore. Pat always wears his favourite green cap out fishing and reckons they will catch a lot of fish when he wears it. The cap is smattered with fish scales. He's nearly always in a good mood, and if the sea is rough and the crew need a lift, he'll start singing, 'Give me a breeze and a good rolling sea'. He particularly likes when

Billy O'Connor is on the boat because his cooking can't be beaten. For his own part, Pat is considered a very good fisherman; a man who can be trusted at all times to do a job properly, especially mending a net. He's a great man to motivate a crew and is a stickler for things being done right and has a strength beyond his small frame. And he's very popular in Dunmore, where he has his own special stoll in a number of the pubs. And with a charming smile and perfect manners, he's very popular with women.

Pat goes to 'The Butchers' every Tuesday night for the traditional Irish music, where he'll have a few Guinness' and small ones.

Pat has never let anyone down in his life and is only going back fishing to help Tomaisín. He's thinking seriously about giving up fishing and settling down. But he'll help Tom with the herrings.

4

The *Honey Dew II* Crew

Tomasz and Aneta Jagly live less than a mile from the Bohans. They are still madly in love; they have been since they first met. Tomasz was sixteen, she was fifteen. For both of them, it feels like only yesterday because it's like time didn't exist before that fateful day. He thought she was gorgeous, she thought he was extremely handsome. When they came to Ireland, Aneta continued to turn heads. Tomasz keeps his hair short, which suits his chiselled features. He first went out on a trawler when he was nineteen and was hooked straight away. In his spare time, he did every available course on fishing. He fished in the Baltic Sea and was out for five days, back in for two, and out again for five. Aneta reckons the seas were much calmer off Poland than they are off Ireland.

He worked as a border guard for a year but he always came

back to fishing. Like his fellow countrymen and women, he heard wages in Ireland were good and because he saw the demise of the fishing industry in Poland, in March 2005 he decided to ring an employment agency in Tralee, and from there Ger Bohan got his name. When he got the phone call from Ger, he decided to come to Kinsale. The two got on well from the first minute they met. Tomasz had some English and with Ger's help it has quickly improved. Tomasz helps translate Ger's instructions to Vladimir and Viktor, the two Lithuanians working with them. He does this through Russian. Tomasz is making more money now than he did in Poland, and even though the cost of living his high, he feels it's a better quality of life than back home.

When he fished in the Baltic Sea, Aneta worried about him and now, when fishing in the Celtic Sea, she worries even more. In the summer of 2005, herself and the two children came over to Ireland for a holiday. Mary Bohan lent them her Ford Galaxy and in three weeks of bliss they toured west Cork, Kerry and Killarney. Aneta hated not being with Tomasz and, in December, they moved over, joining the 200,000 other Polish people living in Ireland. The Jaglys are now renting a nice house in Kinsale. Aneta first worked as a cleaner in the Convent of Mercy, and now helps run a B&B. In November, when the weather was bad, Ger made sure Tomasz was never short of money. Ger has always been very good that way and Tomasz knows he's lucky to be working with such a good skipper.

The Jaglys are really looking forward to Christmas and, like most Polish people, their celebrations centre around the traditional 'supper' at which no meat is served, just fish – twelve dishes, corresponding to the twelve disciples. There's soup (red beetroot), potatoes, herrings, carp and other specialities, much of which is cooked and prepared by Tomasz, who is a qualified chef and loves cooking. For a tall, broad man of 6 ft 3 inches tall, he's very dexterous around the kitchen and the house. He loves fishing, and having been born in Kolobrzeg in northwest Poland near the Baltic Sea, his family has always been involved in the industry in some way. But his greatest love is Aneta, his son Voitek (12) and his daughter Alexandria (8). For Alexandria, her daddy is her 'Prince'.

*

Aside from Tomasz, the *Honey Dew II* has two further crew members, Viktor Losev and Vladimir Kostyr. The two Lithuanian men live in a rented house in another part of Kinsale with some friends. Viktor was born on New Year's Day 1960, and is a fisherman by trade. He is married to Larysa and they have two children, one of whom, their son Dima (17) is travelling over to Ireland with his mother to stay with Viktor for Christmas. Like Tomasz, Viktor has come to Ireland looking to earn more money. He arrived in Ireland in April 2002 and has always fished with Ger Bohan. Ger had heard about Viktor and his vast experience as a boat mechanic through an employment agency in Kerry.

Vladimir came to Ireland in September 2006 and is a friend of Viktor's. He too has experience in fishing and is here for a better life. Both of them know they have a great skipper in Ger Bohan, a great boat in the *Honey Dew II* and a chance to make some money over the coming year. After Viktor's wife and his son return to Lithuania, they will head out fishing with Ger and Tomasz, in the first week in January.

5

December 2006

John Walsh was the coxswain on the lifeboat in Dunmore for thirty years and is now Chairman of the Memorial Wall Committee. It is a wintry December day, threatening rain, as John gets out of his car and contemplates the 172 inscriptions on the Wall, pulling his cap down tighter over his head to ward off the cold. The names may need to be touched up before the next commemoration, in March 2007. John and the other members of the Committee organise the annual gathering to honour those who have lost their lives at sea off the south-east coast. He knows there are some names that must be added now, including those of Glynn Cott and Jan Sankowski, who lost their lives when the *Maggie B* sank off Dunmore in March 2006.

At first glance, the Memorial Wall looks like a war memorial to fallen soldiers. Look closer and you can see that this is a memorial for those who have fought battles not with man, but with nature. The names are there of two teenage cousins, Pat Tobin and PJ Rossiter from Ring, Co. Waterford, who drowned in 1993 while fishing near Helvick Head, a few miles away. Two years later, two Waterford cousins, Edmond Fitzgerald and Paul Dunne, were lost off Ardmore when their 21ft fibreglass boat smashed on rocks. The same year two young canoeists were swept out to sea, Keith Crowley and fourteen-year-old Ros Davies, when the weather had changed very suddenly outside Dunmore. The body of Keith Crowley was later found on the coast of Wales.

John Walsh knows the names of those who died in the *Rising Sun* tragedy on 29 November 2005 will also have to be added: skipper Pat Colfer and his crewmate, Jimmy Meyler, both drowned when the boat sank a few miles from Kilmore Quay. And also to be inscribed is the name of Billy O'Connor, the diver who went down to the sunken vessel to recover Pat's body, which was never found. Something went wrong as Billy was ascending, and he drowned. Finally, Paddy McCabe's name will have to be added to the Wall as well. Paddy was fishing out of Dunmore on the small cockle boat, the *Boyne Harvester*, just a few weeks earlier when he fell into the water and was gone.

Too many names, thinks John Walsh, too many tears in a bitter sea. He knows the stories behind many of the names on the Wall. Near the top is Captain Parle, Harbour Master of Waterford port. He was coming down with another man, Captain Lawlor, to look at Ballyhack Quay when the wind somehow 'caught them' as they were passing Cheekpoint. In an instant the boat capsized, and the two captains drowned; a man from Cheekpoint survived.

Further down the Wall are the names from 1958, when the *Jack*

Buchan sank after leaving Dunmore. The crew of six were just outside the pier when 'a big sea' caught the boat and capsized it. Within seconds, the boat was hurled onto the rocks and broken up like a box of matches. Five men were lost; only one survived. The only reason the survivor made it, John remembers, was that he got a fishing basket between his legs and stayed afloat until a local fishing boat managed to rescue him.

Other tragedies recorded there remain a mystery, such as the night Don Hearne and Joe Rogers were lost from Passage East on Don's boat, the *Mary II*. It was a fine night, no problems anticipated, but their boat sank as they were drifting for herrings. John Hearne, another name up there, was also fishing for herrings when the sea took him. He was coming round Hook Head when the fish shifted on the deck and surged forward to the front of the boat, breaking the bulkhead and sinking the vessel. John Hearne managed to get away from the sinking boat and started swimming toward the rocks just below Hook Lighthouse. One of the lighthouse men rushed down to the water's edge to pull him out, but just as he reached him, John sank. When he resurfaced his head was split open where it had hit a jagged rock. John Hearne didn't survive.

Then there are the names of those who drowned in the *Jenalisa*, in February 1995. John remembers that one well: it was a bad evening and the *Jenalisa* was only twenty minutes from Dunmore, but something happened and the boat capsized. It was that event that prompted John and others to fundraise for a Memorial Wall. One of those others was Kathleen Power, who comes down here every Sunday evening with her husband, Dick. Their fingers follow the outline of their son's name, Niall. For as long as they live, they'll never forget the day the *Jenalisa* went down, taking their son with it.

Niall Power was a tall, handsome, twenty-one-year-old. He was very close to his mother, and was a philosophical young man who talked about death in a relaxed way. 'I think I'm going to die young,' he'd tell his mother, or, if there were some tragic event he'd say, 'It's all in the little black book, Kathleen.'

When Andy Doherty came in that evening and told them Peter Nolan's boat was missing, Kathleen was stuck to the chair; she knew immediately that something terrible had happened. The body of Conor O'Grady was found, but Niall and Peter were never recovered from the sea. The search operation was hampered by terrible storms.

'It always blows a gale when there's a tragedy, I always say that. I don't know why,' says Kathleen. The wreck of the *Jenalisa* was found 3 miles from Dunmore; it was raised, but no bodies were found.

'Over the years, there is just a terrible feeling of helplessness,' says Kathleen. 'I think about him everyday, especially in the house. Not getting the body was the worst as there is no closure, there has never been closure. I come down here once a week to the Wall. It's hard there is no grave, but I still talk to him and we are still waiting. Every time you go down to the beach, you'd always be looking out and thinking . . .'

Kathleen puts her hand up to her neck and rubs the small locket that hangs there: inside a picture of Niall as a child and a picture of Niall before he died. Up in the house, Kathleen and Dick still have his guitar. He loved playing music and writing songs ever since he got his first guitar, when he was only a young lad, the guitar that is still in the shed and was given to him by their friend, Pat Hennessy, who is now fishing on the *Pere Charles*.

The Wall bears testament to the fact that the sea around

Dunmore is a particularly treacherous stretch, where even experienced boat men need to keep their wits about them at all times. And even with that, you can be plain unlucky. Nicko Murphy, a fish buyer and seller and long-time fisherman in Dunmore, says the waters off Dunmore and the Hook are very tricky. He's known boats to 'drop into a deep trough or hole' quite unexpectedly, such is the ferocity caused by a the confluence of waters: waves coming in from the Celtic Sea meeting water coming out of the Waterford estuary and more water coming round from south Wexford. The tides and winds can make it even more turbulent. It's one of the reasons the coastline along Cork, Waterford and Wexford is known as 'the graveyard of a thousand ships'.

John Walsh thinks about next March and the Memorial Service, about the names of the men who must be added to the Wall and remembered, about the grief that lies behind each and every name up there; he hopes it's going to be a kind winter.

*

Tom Hennessy and Denis Harding get into Dunmore on 15 December, which is the last day before Christmas for landings for the Fishermen's Co-Op. They unload their final catches for 2006. Everything stops now for the Christmas break, and fishing won't resume until 8 January at least, and then with the herrings.

Ger Bohan, with his *Honey Dew* crew, and Johnny Walsh, with his *Rachel Jay* crew, arrive into Kinsale on 16 December. The fish buyers stop buying around this time because they want all the fish in cold storage for Christmas. The next few weeks will be expensive for all the fishermen as most will have no income at all for the next fortnight. Therefore when the first 'window of

46

opportunity' opens up in January, they'll be going at it hard. The past two months have been particularly bad for fishing; the *Honey Dew* rarely got out in November ('a wipe-out', says Mary) and December wasn't much better, so there's a lot of hope pinned on the weather being kind in January and the fishing being good.

Over the Christmas period the body of Paddy McCabe, who fell from the *Boyne Harvester*, is washed up on the Welsh coast – more than three weeks after he went missing outside Dunmore. It offers some comfort to his family.

There's joy in Lulu Doyle's house over Christmas as the children are delighted with what Santa brings – and Lulu is thrilled with what Tom has given her: a beautiful engagement ring. He gave her a 'first' engagement ring many years ago, but now he wants them to get married, sometime in 2007 he reckons. On St Stephen's Day, Tom, Lulu, Christine and Jane go to Kerry for a few days. Tom says something strange, something he's never spoken about before: 'Lu, when I die I want to be buried in Kerry.' Lulu starts crying. She loves him more than she can say. She can't imagine living without him.

Over in Kinsale, the Bohans have one of the nicest Christmases ever. It's great to have Ger around. On St Stephen's Day, Ger decides he wants to get all the documentation for the safety equipment for the boat together. He gathers up all the various bits of paper, puts it in a single file and places it in the front room.

'Sure, it's all in there now, in case you're ever looking for it,' he says to Mary.

Mary Bohan's relations from Bantry arrive on New Year's Eve, along with cousins and friends from England. That evening, Anthony babysits while Ger, Mary and the other adults go to the White Lady pub, where local singer Ronnie Costely is belting out

Niall Diamond, Frank Sinatra and Elvis hits. Once the crowd gets going in the White Lady, Mary and Ger start dancing; everybody is dancing. They have a great night and hold each other close as midnight approaches. On the stroke of midnight, the cheers ring out as Ger plants a big kiss on Mary's lips.

'Roll on 2007,' he says, 'it can't get any worse.'

PART II

LOST AT SEA

6

The Herring Season

Denis Harding has the *Suzanna G* 'changed over' to fish for herrings because, as Denis knows, January is normally a good month for herrings as they are spawning and therefore easier to locate and kill. Tom Hennessy tells Michael Walsh that as soon as the weather breaks, they'll go fishing for herrings; Michael says he will ring the co-ordinator in Cork to 'book in' the *Pere Charles* and the *Suzanna G* for pair-fishing from 8 January.

There are severe gales on Tuesday, 2 January after what has been a dirty winter so far. In Kinsale, Ger Bohan decides not to go fishing, but is anxious to get the year off to a good start. The following day he takes a look at the weather and decides to go out. It's drizzling and the forecast is for south-westerly, fresh to strong and gusty winds for later in the day; they might even reach gale force at times. It's bad, but not too bad. He gets his crew together – Tomasz, Viktor and Vladimir – and they head out. The skipper of the *Rachel Jay*, Johnny Walsh, is on holidays the first week of January, so his relief skipper, Roger Murphy, goes out instead. The *Honey Dew* and the *Rachel Jay* are not herring fishing; they are fishing for 'white fish', such as cod, monk, hake, plaice. They will fish separately off the Waterford coast, but Ger and Roger will talk to each other regularly to see how things are going.

While Ger is out fishing, Tom Hennessy is looking forward to starting his fishing season on Monday, 8 January. The money the crew got from Michael Walsh before Christmas from their two nights of herring fishing worked out at €300 each. Tom thought it was good money; he certainly never expected to get as much from just two trips. There's not as big an expense with herring fishing as there is with trawling for white fish as the boat is not going away for an extended period. It just goes out past the Hook; the fuel bill is very manageable – €100 a night easily covers it; there's no need for ice; and there are no big food bills. A trip to the Smalls, off Cornwall, for example, searching for white fish can cost up to €4,000 for four days, but for herring fishing the *Pere Charles* can be run for €1,000 for the entire week. That means, of course, that there will be more money to share out.

At home, Lulu is enjoying having Tom around the house for a change and isn't looking forward to the start of the season. He teases her that she is supposed to be encouraging him to go to work and earn some money, not trying to keep him on shore.

*

On Saturday morning, 6 January, Marco Power from Dunmore gives his friend Billy O'Connor a lift up to the village. Marco is in his early twenties and gets on well with Billy, whom he knows as 'Billy Squid'. They don't live far from each other. Billy tells Marco that he's going out herring fishing with Tomaisín (as they call Tom Hennessy), maybe from Sunday night as their licence for the week runs from Sunday afternoon to 2.00pm the following Friday.

'Well, if you need a hand any night, I'll go out,' Marco tells Billy. Billy says he'll let Tomaisín know there's an extra pair of hands for hire. Marco has known Tomaisín since he arrived in Dunmore and regards him as a very good fisherman. He also knows the *Pere Charles* and has been on it a few times in the harbour, but has yet to get out fishing in it.

Billy tells Tom that Marco is interested in going fishing, but a few hours later Marco decides he won't go and rings Tomaisín to tell him he won't be taking up the offer of the berth.

'No bother,' says Tomaisín, 'give me a ring if you change your mind.'

That Saturday evening, at the same time as Marco is talking to Tomaisín, Pat Coady is having a drink in Whites of Ballymacaw, near Dunmore, with his girlfriend, Sarah Maher. Their daughter, Treasa, is now five. Pat tells Sarah that he's going out fishing on the *Suzanna G* with Denis Harding and is really looking forward to it. He's so excited at the prospect, he can't stop talking about it.

On Sunday, Tom rings around to see who will go out with him. Some men aren't interested in the hard work. Lulu can hear him on the phone and recognises some of the names, but she knows that crews change a lot and there's no set pattern to it. By Sunday evening, Tom has got what he considers a great crew together, 'a dream team'.

Monday, 8 January: Tom Hennessy and Denis Harding have until 2.00pm on Friday afternoon to catch herrings. Met Eireann is forecasting bad weather for Wednesday night, Thursday and Friday, so their 'window of opportunity' starts now and there's no time to lose. On Monday, they check the boats and the gear. There won't be any other Dunmore boats going out for herrings this week because it doesn't pay them to make the changes to equip the vessels and because the quota is now so strict. Both the *Pere Charles* and the *Suzanna G* have been given a quota of 70 tonnes each for herring for the week, which means they can catch 140 tonnes between them. If they don't catch that 140 tonnes, they won't be allowed to 'carry it over' to next week. The men estimate that if they get close to 140 tonnes, the price should be good enough to make it a profitable week.

The boats will be pair-fishing for the week: Tom will skipper the *Pere Charles*; Denis will be at the controls of the *Suzanna G*. When working in pairs, it's important that the skippers know and trust one another. Denis has known Tom since he first came to Dunmore and regards him highly. He knows Tom is a well-liked skipper who commands great respect from his crew. And Denis knows the crew, too. He has fished with Billy O'Connor and thinks he's a great character. He's had drinks with Pat Hennessy and knows he's everyone's darling, that he's like the Lord Mayor in the Butcher's pub sometimes. Denis loves the way Pat tells stories, with his soft, Kerry accent, a bit like the great Frank Kelly. He knows Andrey to see and knows that if Tom has him on his boat, he must be good.

The weather forecast for the next few days is unsettled, which is no surprise as it's coming after months of unsettled weather. The low pressure over the country is continuing, caused by deep Atlantic depressions rolling in over Ireland. Since 10 November there have been consistently high waves along the Irish coast, generally above 3m (10ft) and sometimes up to 8m (26ft).

Meteorologists know that a certain amount of the energy from these waves is lost as they approach the coast, but because it gets shallower, the energy tends to increase. This energy has to go somewhere, and normally it goes up, making the waves steeper. Also, tidal currents can create a lot more confusion in certain areas, where waves bounce off the coast and come back, meeting other waves on the way in. Sometimes if a boat is closer to the coast, it can be a lot more difficult to handle because the sea can be a lot more 'confused', as the men say. Waves further offshore can be more predictable because fishermen can see them coming, whereas closer to the shore they can come out of nowhere. This is what fishermen refer to as a 'good lump' in the sea.

Tom and Denis check everything, including the wooden boards in the hold of each boat that will keep the fish in each separate compartment, or 'pound'. The pound boards are made of heavy deal and have marks cut into the timber, numbering each one, so the crew knows which board slots on top of the other. The boards are slightly rounded at the edge so they can be lifted up when necessary. The stanchions holding them in place are made of steel. Fishing will begin tomorrow.

Tuesday, 9 January: little Treasa Coady knows her Daddy is going fishing today. Sarah gets up for work and gets Treasa ready for school. Pa gives his daughter a kiss and tells her he'll be late home that night. She waves goodbye as she goes off with her Mammy. Pa knows he's fishing tonight and probably tomorrow, and doesn't know if he'll get a chance either night to tuck her in or read her a story. He's going to miss her the days he's out there. After a while he gets up, smokes a Benson & Hedges, gets his stuff together and drives down to the quay. He parks the car and meets up with Denis Harding and the other crew members on the

Suzanna G, on which Coady is due to work for the next few days. Denis also has Brian Crummy and two Lithuanian men on board.

On the *Pere Charles*, Tom has his uncle Pat with him, Billy 'the Squid' O'Connor and Andrey Dyrin. He rings Brian Murphy, whom he knows, and asks if he and Darren Walsh want to come along. Both are on the quay at the time and say, 'Why not?' Tom brings the vessel over to where they are and they jump on. The boat now has six men on board, a good crew. Both boats head out around 12.30pm.

The herring fishing is not great that day and the nets get damaged during the evening. Brian and Darren spend much of the day in the wheelhouse with Tom, chatting about this and that. They have only caught a few tonnes of fish by the time they call it a night. They arrive back in Dunmore around 10.00pm. Brian Murphy has told Tom that he won't be going out herring fishing tomorrow because he's fishing on the *Ludovic Geoffray* in a few hours time, at 4.00am. Darren Walsh tells him he won't be going out either. So now Tom has a problem because at the moment there's only him and three others going out on the *Pere Charles* the following morning and it's not enough. He'll ask Denis if Pa Coady can switch and join him for the day.

*

The *Honey Dew II* steamed back into Kinsale on Monday night, 8 January. Ger and the lads have been out since Wednesday and have netted 'a nice bit of cod'. Ger is feeling good, it's a positive start to the year. The weather wasn't great out there, but it was manageable. Aneta Jagly is on the quay with her two children to greet Tomasz as the boat comes home.

After unloading the fish onto a lorry that will take it to the markct in Skibbereen, Ger locks the boat and drives home. Viktor and Vladimir get a lift to their house. Ger gets in at 10.30pm, 'rank with the dirt'. Mary is delighted to see him, as are the children the following morning. He spends a bit of time with them, then heads back down to the quay to check out a few things on the boat.

At around 10.00am he rings Mary and asks her to join him in Cucinas for a nice breakfast of scrambled eggs. Just after they sit down to eat, Ger's mobile phone rings. It's a naval officer calling from Navy HQ in Haulbawline in Cork to ask about his where-abouts and why the VMS1[2] has been turned off. Ger gets annoyed. He tells the man he's having breakfast in a restaurant in Kinsale and that the boat is a few hundred yards away, tied up at the pier. The officer says the 'blip' on his computer screen indicating where the *Honey Dew* is had just 'disappeared'. Ger says he'll be back down the pier in a short while and he'll check it out then. He hangs up just as his two friends, Johnny Walsh and Eamonn O'Neill, come in the door. He tells them about the call. A little later Ger wonders aloud about what they will do with the few thousand euro they will get from the special government savings scheme, the SSIA. He says to Mary, 'We'll have to go down to Paschal and get things sorted out once and for all with the insurance.'

---

[2] VMS is a Vessel Monitoring System, which lets the Irish Navy know where any Irish trawler is at any given time or any other EU fishing vessel operating within Irish waters. Every Irish fishing vessel over 15m has to have a VMS satellite transponder or 'box' which sends a signal every 2 hours to the Fisheries Monitoring Centre at Navy HQ in Haulbawline in Cork, who then know where each boat is. The information contains course of speed, position, date and time. The system is not used for safety but is used to implement and aid fisheries management at sea. If a trawler

Ger had been talking about putting more money into his life assurance policy for some time, but has never got around to it. Now, on this Tuesday morning in January, he wants to do something about it. After their breakfast, Ger goes in to his friend, insurance broker Paschal Kiely, and says, 'Can you upgrade our life policy and upgrade our pensions please, Paschal?' Paschal tells Ger to leave it with him and to call up next week, when he's back in from fishing.

Johnny Walsh has everything ready for his boat, the 22m *Rachel Jay*, and he and his crew head out to fish at midday. The winds are south-westerly, moderate to strong. Ger will go back out on Wednesday morning.

*

In Dunmore, Tom and Denis agree they'll have to get one of the nets mended for the morning if they're to go out again. Pat Hennessy is very quick at mending: it's his forte. Coady knows it will be late by the time they are finished mending the net, so he rings Sarah around 10.00pm, when they get in to Dunmore, to say they're only just back and as they are going out early the next morning, he's going to sleep on the *Suzanna G*. She says she'll see him tomorrow.

---

is in port, an Irish skipper can turn off his VMS but he must inform Navy HQ. Or if it is powered down (if work is being carried out on a boat) fishermen are also to ring Navy HQ to tell them. There are on average 400-500 fishing boats in Irish waters each day and approx. 10,000 VMS 'signals' are received by Navy HQ over a 24-hour period. There can be up to 15 'missed reports' every day, always Irish vessels as Irish skippers are the only ones who are able to turn off their VMS. Other countries don't allow their skippers this facility.

They unload the small amount of herrings they have caught and mend the net.

When they're finished, Billy O'Connor walks up the hill to his home. It's 12.20am when he puts his key in the door. He's tired; it has been a long day. Mary is still up, waiting for him. Billy puts four herrings in the fridge, which he filleted earlier in the day; he knows Mary will like them for her breakfast. Billy tells her the lads are looking for someone else for the morning as one of the crew can't make it. 'Sure, they won't get anybody else at this time of night,' he says to her.

She asks him does he need anything for the morning. 'A sliced pan and my pillow,' he replies wearily. The lads had eaten all the bread on board that day and more would be needed for sandwiches or toast tomorrow. He needs his pillow in case he gets a chance to put his head down for an hour during the day. He tells her they have to be back at the boat at 6.00am as they are leaving early. Mary takes a sliced pan out of the freezer and they go to bed.

Over at Tom Hennessy's house, Christine and Jane are fast asleep and Lulu is in bed when he arrives home after midnight. He'd been gone since early that morning. Lulu knows the new regulations mean that once Tom signed in for herring fishing for the week, he couldn't go fishing for white fish. Before, he could chop and change depending on how the weather was and the conditions. She thinks Tom prefers being out at the whitefish, but as the weather is going to be bad for the next couple of weeks, she knows he'd prefer to be at the herrings than sitting around, doing nothing.

He gives her a kiss and says, 'Lu, I'm just wrecked, I'll see you in the morning, I have to be up before six.'

Tom sets his alarm for 5.45am and goes to sleep.

7

A Confused Sea

Wednesday morning, 10 January 2007.

The sun won't rise over Dunmore until nearly 8.00am. Billy O'Connor's alarm goes off at 5.30am and he forces himself out of bed before he has a chance to fall back asleep. Mary gets up and puts on her dressing-gown. She always gets up when he's going out fishing so early. While he's washing and getting dressed, she gets things ready for the fry and puts on the kettle. Billy likes a cup of tea and a fry on a morning like this; it sets him up for the day. By 5.45am, he is ready to go; it will only take him ten or fifteen minutes to walk down to the quay. Mary gets his pillow and the sliced pan and puts them in his hold-all. Billy says he's not going to take his mobile phone with him. It's the one the children got him for Christmas and it's too good to have on the boat. He puts on his old, black, leather jacket and heads for the door. Mary notices his hair is getting long.

'I'll have to cut that hair,' she tells him. 'I'll cut it when you get back in tonight.'

He laughs, says okay and opens the front door. It's a calm, quiet morning, not a puff of wind.

'Lovely,' says Billy, 'we'll get a good bit of fishing done today.'

'When you get back, will you have the dinner?' asks Mary. Billy says no, he won't, he'll make something for the lads on the way in and they'll all have their dinner on the boat. He gives her a kiss and says goodbye. Mary is standing on the front step.

'Go in now or you'll get cold,' he tells her.

She says goodbye and waves as he walks down the driveway with his pillow and his sliced pan, crossing the shadows created by the streetlight. Mary goes in and fries up the four herrings; she loves fresh herrings.

Tom Hennessy's alarm goes off at 5.45am. He gets up very quietly, so as not to wake Lulu, and gets dressed. Lulu would normally get up to make tea for him when he is going out early, and this is the first morning in a long time he doesn't wake her. Just before he leaves, he turns and gives her a soft kiss, then quietly walks out the door. Gone to fish.

Down on the pier, Pa Coady lifts his head from his pillow in the bunk of the *Suzanna G.* He hears noises up on deck: must be time to get up and get going, he thinks. The two boats are due to leave shortly. It's a nice morning, good weather. The break in the weather is continuing and Met Eireann is predicting a fine spell for the morning and afternoon, although he heard last night that it will get nasty later in the evening. He gets up and has a cigarette.

When Denis Harding arrives, Tom asks him if he can have one

of his lads for the day. Coady's name is mentioned because Tom knows Coady is one of the most experienced men at the herrings. If Coady can't work on the *Pere Charles* today, Tom will have to get somebody else, probably Lulu's brother-in-law, Lee. Denis knows Coady will do a good job for Tom on the *Pere Charles*. Denis likes Coady, always has. He is a very experienced fisherman, even though he's only twenty-seven. He asks Coady will he go over and work on the *Pere Charles* for the day. Coady agrees, goes down below and gets his bag and his few bits and pieces and leaves the *Suzanna G.* He jumps over onto the deck of the *Pere Charles* for what they all hope will be a good day's fishing.

Like yesterday, Denis and Tom will be communicating via the VHF radio on channel P4. In a way, it's their personal channel. Most other boats won't be using that channel, so it allows for one-to-one communication. The only voice Tom is likely to hear is Denis' and vice versa.

The rest of the crew arrive and before dawn both vessels are heading out of Dunmore. Tom and Denis listen to the early morning Sea Area forecast on the radio. Last night they were told that an unstable south-west airflow was covering the country, that a gale warning was in operation and that there was a warning of heavy sea swells, mainly off the west coast. Met Eireann predicts the 'state of the sea' to be rough rising to very rough, particularly for sea crossings from Rosslare and Cork to France. It doesn't sound great, but it doesn't sound awful either: they'll manage.

*

The weather forecasts are a fisherman's lifeline – they listen intently to the regular updates and usually plot their day's fishing accordingly. Met Eireann gets a lot of its information on sea state from its six navigational buoys dotted around the coast. These buoys are around the size of a small car. Like a big beach ball bobbing in the sea, these 3mx3m yellow markers have a white flashing light at the top, are made of steel and are anchored to the seabed. Inside each one there is a lot of equipment, which is all duplicated in case something breaks down. So there are two thermometers, two barometers, two anemometers and two wave sensors. The thermometers measure the temperature; the barometers measure the pressure; the anemometers measure the speed and direction of the wind (they are connected to wind vanes attached to the top of the buoy); and the wave sensors measure wave height and wave period, i.e. the time lapse between each wave.

On top of each buoy are two antennae, which send the information, via satellite, to Darmstadt in Germany, the main weather information-gathering centre in Europe. Darmstadt sends it back to the various national met offices in each country. Five of the six buoys are 30 miles off the coast because this is traditionally how far a sea area forecast will cover; they are located off counties Galway, Dublin, Kerry, Donegal and Wexford. The sixth buoy is 200 miles out into the Atlantic, off the west coast, and has a 3km rope/chain holding it in place. For the forecasters in Met Eireann, it's a great achievement to have a buoy so far out. The information it provides helps the office to supply a longer-range forecast.

The height of a wave is measured from the crest (top) to the trough (bottom) and is the vertical distance between the two. People who study waves talk about 'significant' wave height, which is the average height of the highest one-third of the wave. For example, a 'calm' sea will have wave heights of 0–0.1m (0–0.32ft). 'Wavelets' are the next level, followed by 'Slight' sea, which can have waves of up to 1.25m (4ft). Then seas can become 'Moderate',

'Rough' (2.5–4m/8–13ft) and 'Very Rough' (4–6m/13–19ft). 'High Seas' have waves of between 6m and 9m (19–29ft) in height, and 'Very High Seas' have waves 9–14m (29–46ft).

All of these 'scientific' measurements are very close to the visual estimates of wave heights given by experienced seamen. The last wave type is something no seafarer ever wants to experience: 'Phenomenal'. These are waves that are over 14m (46ft) high. Considering that the height of a double-deck bus is 4.4m (14.3ft), waves that are over 14m will be roughly the equivalent of three double-deck buses stacked one on top of the other – an awesome and fearful sight.

Of course, what must be remembered is these are average measurements of waves. Within all these calculations, individual waves will exceed the average height in any of the categories given above. So if the weather forecaster predicts that there will be 'High Seas' when waves should be 'only' between 6m and 9m (19ft and 29ft) high, in that you will get some waves that will reach maybe 10m (32.8ft) – and that's only in 'High Seas'.

For Tom Hennessy and Denis Harding on the morning of 10 January, the prediction is that south-west or strong gales will develop on Wednesday evening and early Wednesday night on all sea areas. Winds may even reach storm force and are expected to reach Force 6 at times on all coasts later in the evening or night. The state of the sea is predicted to go from Rough to Very Rough to High, and there's a warning of heavy swells on north-west, west and south-west coasts. Strong Force 9 winds are expected after dark, possibly reaching storm Force 10. For now, though, that's all in the future. Looking out from the wheelhouse this morning, it's not too bad as the boats chart a course that will bring them south of Hook Head.

*

The first thing the *Pere Charles* and the *Suzanna G* have to do is find the fish.

Older fishermen in the Suir estuary say there remains a shroud of mystery surrounding the herring, even with all the latest technology. It's still not known, for example, when exactly a herring shoal will arrive, or why it might go to a particular location. It's also not known when they will spawn (deposit their eggs), or where they go after spawning. What is known is that the waters off Dunmore East and the Hook are normally good herring fishing grounds, particularly in January.

Using the echo sounder, they see a shoal of herrings underneath, maybe 2m (6.5ft) from the seabed. The herrings are spawning. Tom marks the co-ordinates on the plotter and tells the crew to get ready. They shoot one end of the net from the *Pere Charles*. The *Suzanna G* pulls up alongside and the crew on the *Pere Charles* toss over the throwing line, which is hauled in and secured.

Tom and Denis push down lightly on the throttles and keep level with each other as they reach a speed of 3 knots. They stay at this speed, and at a constant distance, and will tow the net through their 'mark'.

Herrings are very fast swimmers; if they see the net, they'll move, scatter, in the blink of an eye. If the boats miss the herrings, they have to turn around and come back again. But the towing process only takes five to ten minutes and today, the fishing should be good. They plan to shoot three times and haul three times, with hopefully thousands of herrings in each haul.

When a bag with all the fish comes onto the deck, the herrings are hosed down and shovelled into the hatch and onto the pounds below. The small, hard, slippery fish flow into the front, or forid, pound (normally on the left, or port, side) and the pound boards are slipped into place to hold them there. The first pound is 'one board low', so when the fish reach the ceiling, they spill over into the next pound; when this fills up, they spill into the next pound and so on. There will always be one, possibly two, men down in the hatch to shift a board and make sure everything is filling up nicely.

Denis and Tom know the tides today are 3.7m (12ft) – not too strong. The tides will have been getting slacker, too, because they were strongest on 6 January, at 4.1m (13ft). (You will notice on a beach that some tides bring the water miles out: these are called 'spring' tides because they come further in and go further out; others, which are less than 4m, are known as slack tides. 'Spring tides' are the ones with the largest tidal ranges and come about at new moon and full moon, whereas 'neap tides' have the smallest tidal ranges and come about at first and third quarter of the lunar monthly cycle).

Michael Walsh, owner of the *Pere Charles*, is heading to Cork for a meeting of the Celtic Sea Herring Management Committee, which is due to discuss the state of herring fishing along the south and south-east coasts. He rings Tom to ask him how things are going. Tom tells him things are going great; 'And you'll never believe who we have on with us? We have Coady with us.'

'Great, you've got an experienced man there,' says Michael. They chat for a while and Michael says he'll talk to him later.

Tom and Denis make the first haul. It's a good one – maybe 27 tonnes of herring. The herring net is taken onto the stern of the *Pere Charles*, as this is where the hatch is, where the shelter deck is and where the men work. Tom's crew pour the fish down the small hole into the pounds below. It takes around forty-five minutes from the time the net is on deck to the time the fish are all down below. While the crew on the *Pere Charles* are busy doing this, there's not much to do on the *Suzanna G* so the men sit down and have a coffee, some have a cigarette, one or two might even go down below for a snooze. Denis stays at the wheel. The way the net has been lifted in means he is now behind the *Pere Charles*. He watches as Coady, Pat, Billy and Andrey empty the net. After a while, the net is ready to go back into the water. Tom and Denis talk on the VHF and the net goes back down as the hunt for herring continues.

The men are enjoying the work. On the *Pere Charles*, Tom Hennessy is delighted with the catch so far, particularly as yesterday's catch was so small. He's delighted with the crew, too, they are playing their part with great dedication.

Pat Coady thinks it's brilliant; he smokes another cigarette and laughs and jokes with the other men. He's thrilled to be back fishing, especially with such a good bunch of lads. It'll be a nice few bob to tide him over before he goes back on the diggers. And even if it wasn't a great haul, he would still love just being out here.

Pat Hennessy just loves this type of day – when the fish are coming in and everybody is pulling together; he takes some Drum tobacco from his packet and rolls himself a cigarette. Andrey Dyrin is amazed to see so much fish. This is one of the best day's fishing he has ever been on. Fishing for cod or haddock is one thing, but hitting a good shoal of herrings is something else. He'll be able to send Natalya some extra money, or put it towards the flight and the journey back to Ukraine.

Meanwhile, Michael Walsh is in deep discussion with other members of the Celtic Sea Herring Committee about the rule that trawlers can't fish herrings and whitefish in the same week, that it must be one or the other. Michael tells the meeting that the fishermen he represents are complaining about it because herrings are just a top-up, and you can't have one without the other. During a short break he rings Tom from the meeting room to see if he is going to book in at the herrings for the following week. Tom tells them they're having a great day so far.

'Look it, I'll leave it with yourself,' Michael tells him, 'you have to book in if you want to come; if we don't book in, we won't be herring fishing next week.'

When Tom hangs up, he thinks about it and about the excellent first haul of herrings. He rings Michael and says, 'Stick us in for next week again.' Michael knows from Tom's voice that he's on a high and that all the crew are 'on the buzz'. He knows that if they catch their 140-tonne quota in the space of two days, each crew member will have €600 for their two days' work, which is the equivalent of five or six days out at the Smalls. He can tell they are enjoying the work, and the prospect of the extra money.

*

Ger Bohan is heading out past the Old Head of Kinsale, ready for what he hopes will be another good five days of fishing. He knows the weather is due to turn bad tonight, but he has been out in bad weather before and has great faith in the *Honey Dew*. He also has a hard-working crew in Tomasz and the two boys. Aneta drove Tomasz down to the quay, as usual. They kissed and he said he'd be back in four or five days, and will call her tomorrow.

As they head further out to sea, Ger radios his old friend Johnny Walsh, who's out here on the *Rachel Jay*, and they have a good chat. The previous evening, Ger spoke with Phil Devitt, the

Harbour Master in Kinsale, to tell him he was heading out this morning and will be out for a few days. Phil doesn't envy Ger the job he has to do. Every week, Phil sees the increasing financial pressure Ger and other fishermen are under. It's a job he's glad he doesn't have to do himself. Nonetheless, he knows men like Ger are born fishermen, happy to be heading out, eyes fixed on the horizon and the freedom of the waves; and even happier when coming home with a good catch.

*

Off Hook Head, Tom is taking in the second haul of herrings. As the net comes in, the lads realise this second haul is as big, if not bigger, than the first one. The crews are delighted; Tom and Denis are smiling. Again, the net goes onto the *Pere Charles* and the fish are packed into the pounds down below. It's hard work for Pat, Andrey, Coady and Billy. All the pounds are now full and Tom reckons he has between 50 and 60 tonnes of herring on board. He gets on the radio to Denis.

'She's full now,' says Tom. The *Pere Charles* is full after the first two shots. The *Suzanna G* is behind the *Pere Charles* and from his wheelhouse, Denis can't see beyond its shelter deck. He doesn't know if Tom has herrings on the deck, which he would have to do if there were no more room down below. Denis knows Tom is really pleased with the catch. Tom is in a great mood; he'll ring Lulu's brother-in-law, Lee, on shore in a while and because they're 'stuffed' with herrings, he'll ask him to come down later to give them a hand unloading them as there will be a lot of herrings to be dug out.

'We've enough now,' Tom says to Denis, 'we've no more room for any more, you take the last load. We've two options, we can go in now and the two crews get around this one and dig them out quick, and if it's fine tomorrow, we can go back out; or if we shoot again, you can take the herrings.'

They know the weather is due to deteriorate in a few hours, but it's still early in the afternoon, not yet 2.00pm. It doesn't take them long to make a decision – they'll go for the third shot and be back in Dunmore before the weather.

Pat Coady's mobile rings. It's Sarah, asking what time does he think he'll be in. Pat isn't sure. He tells her he's on the *Pere Charles* as they were a man short.

'You should see the fish here, Sarah,' he says. 'There's some fish out here. I'm not sure what time we'll be in, but I'll be home to put Treasa to bed.'

'Okay, see you later,' says Sarah.

*

Michael Walsh comes out of his meeting and rings Tom, who tells him the *Pere Charles* is full and they are going to shoot the nets and get a haul for the *Suzanna G.* Michael says he's leaving Cork soon and will stop at Dunmore en route to his home in Arthurstown, across the River Suir. Tom says he is going to ring the fishery officer in Dunmore to tell him that they'll be in around 6.00pm.

Michael isn't worried about the weather closing in on them; nor is Tom – they have loads of time. In general, fishermen keep working until the weather comes on. It's not a case of listening to the forecast and deciding not to go out; most times a skipper will head out, fish away and only when a gale of wind comes on will he then start heading for home. Why? Because the boats are capable of working and travelling in bad weather. Anybody who watches television programmes about trawling or deep-sea fishing will see this, as they will see that fishermen throw out and haul nets in bad, or even very bad, weather. The fishing doesn't stop when the wind rises and the rain pours. That's one of the reasons why Ger Bohan is now out at his fishing grounds, ready to trawl. He reckons he'll be hauling in his nets later as well. He knows the weather will be bad by then, but he's been out in bad weather before.

It's not a case that boats aren't supposed to go out in gales of wind. Sail boats, for example, have been crossing the Atlantic for centuries. Boats are built for handling the sea in bad weather, and it's not until a boat hits really bad weather that a fisherman knows how good it is. Tom knows this is especially true of French boats, like the *Pere Charles*, because French fishermen stay out working in bad weather a lot of the time. The *Pere Charles* was built to work a long way from home; it wasn't built to run away from Force 7, 8 or 9 winds.

At the same time though, fishermen are always very conscious of tuning into the weather forecasts and listening hard to interpret it for themselves. For example, a fisherman will try to judge how the wind is going to be and how exactly the weather patterns will affect the particular area in which he is fishing in order to anticipate how bad it will get in his local area. A fisherman is always aware of how far he is from port, and if it gets too bad, what side the weather will be on as he makes for land. Tom and Denis off the Hook, like Ger and Johnny off west Waterford, are always focused on such matters.

*

In the Met Eireann offices, the weather forecasters are assessing the data and reckoning that it's going to be a rough night. Their information is coming in from weather charts, from their six buoys around the coast, from the weather equipment on the Marathon oil and gas platform south of Cork, from their weather stations around the country and from satellite and radar sources. What they can see is a depression just south of Iceland, bringing with it a frontal system that is passing over Ireland as a strong, gale force, south-westerly airflow. This frontal system is pushing lots of wind in its path, along with rain and squally showers, and it should reach the south coast of Ireland around midnight. The problem is that there is a division between two air masses. The old air is sweeping up from Iceland and colliding with the warm air that is already over Ireland. This means the weather will be 'confused,' with rain and unpredictable gusts of wind.

A cold front coming from the south-west can become a vicious beast as it races across the land and sea, with strong winds ahead of it, in it and chasing after it. The winds will be shifting within the front as well, which means as it passes over a town, or a boat, the wind can change suddenly. It may be pushing winds from a southerly direction ahead of it, but then it might shift to a westerly direction as it passes, after which it may bring north-west winds.

A weather front can move at a speed of 30 knots and can bring dramatic changes to a sea area in the space of less than one hour. The previous day, 9 January, was a very windy day, generating waves 5–6m (16–19ft) high off the Kerry coast, and it has 'left over' some sea that is now getting ready to pick up again: waves are lurking with intent or, as some fishermen say, are bubbling under the surface with energy and hate. The information coming into Met Eireann for Wednesday morning shows that wind speeds are already up to 20 knots in some places; with the waves still fairly big from the previous day, this will increase the wave height even more.

The strength and power of a wave depends on how strong the wind is blowing, how long it's been blowing and the distance over which the wind is blowing, which is known as the 'fetch' of the wind. Sometimes fishermen and scientists speak of a 'confused sea', meaning a sea that doesn't really know what it's doing due to variations in the shape and direction of the waves. Then the wind might die down, at which point the waves the wind made are called 'swell'. So the wind might have dropped off, but the waves keep on coming. These are the waves that can run for days with very little loss of energy.

Meteorologists believe storm waves tend not to last very long, but smooth, streamlined waves with definite crests and troughs and a more rhythmic rise and fall can persist for a very long time, travelling hundreds, even thousands, of miles. And of course these waves interact with each other as well, with faster waves overtaking slower ones, thus reinforcing or cancelling each other out. Despite appearances, a wave is not a ridge of water travelling on the surface of the sea. Rather, it is a manifestation of the energy from the wind, which has been translated into circular movements of water molecules. The easiest way to understand this is to imagine a crowd performing a Mexican wave. The wave appears to move sideways around the sport stadium, when in fact each person moves up and down. The Japanese word for a 'harbour wave' is tsunami because it is only when it reaches shore that this type of wave manifests itself and causes havoc; it might have been only 1m (3ft) high when out in the remote ocean deep.

Although it's a commonly held belief, a wave doesn't have to be massive to cause damage. If a boat is very laden and very low in the water and a 2m or 3m (6ft or 9ft) wave catches it at the wrong angle, it could cause the boat to list heavily to one side. If another wave then rolls in before the boat has managed to right itself, the results can be catastrophic.

The other type of wave is that created during wild storms. Within what meteorologists define as a 'Phenomenal storm', there might be individual waves of 30m (98ft). Statistics show that one in every 3,000 waves will be twice the significant wave height. In an Atlantic storm with significant wave heights of, say, 7m, this means there will be a 14m (46ft) wave every eight or nine hours, assuming that the time lapse between each wave (the wave period) is about 10–12 seconds. Scientists have worked out that 'in a normal situation', 15 per cent of the waves will be twice the average height. This is why some people talk about the seventh wave being bigger than the rest because, statistically one in seven waves (15 per cent) will exceed the average.

If that is not bad enough, the height of a wave is not as important as its steepness. A boat can ride a high wave if the wave is, for example, very long: it climbs up one side and slides down the other. But if a wave is steep, the boat could be in trouble. The boat can climb up, but the stern of the vessel can get hung on one crest while the front, or bow, is driven into the next wave as it comes crashing forward. Very importantly, waves tend to get steeper during the earlier part of a storm than later, when the sea is more fully developed.

Another important measurement is how quickly waves race towards the boat. This is known as the wave period: the time lapse between two successive crests passing a given point. In storms, it might only be a second or two from the time the first wave hits to the time the next wave hits, and that pounding sequence can last for hours. In less stormy seas, the speed of the waves decreases a little, but they can still hit a boat every five to ten seconds.

The most terrifying wave in the sea's repertoire is the rogue, or freak, wave. It is defined as 'a wave which is more than twice the significant wave height'. For the fisherman, this means a huge volume of water approaching that is completely unexpected. The first rogue wave measured directly was that which hit an oil platform in the North Sea in 1985 and was an awe-inspiring 19m (63ft) high. Then in 2000 a rogue wave measuring 29.1m (96ft) was witnessed off Rockall after a westerly wind had been blowing for two days. In 1996 the *QE2* luxury liner was hit by a 29m (95ft) freak wave, which crew members described as 'horrific and monstrous'. The cause of rogue waves is a matter of debate, but some scientists believe the wave 'steals' energy from its immediate neighbours. What is certain, however, is that rogue waves are now far more common than was thought even ten years ago.

*

It's nearly 4.00 in the afternoon and Denis and Tom shoot for their third and final catch of herrings. They spot a shoal and within five minutes the net is straining again, full of herrings. Both vessels now have their lights on as it's getting dark quickly. The beam from Hook Head lighthouse strobes across the rolling Celtic Sea, one of the oldest lighthouses in the world. Denis is going to take this haul, so they manoeuvre the boats close to each other. The heavy net of herrings comes onto the *Suzanna G* on its starboard side as the shelter deck on this boat is to the bow, not to the stern as it is on the *Pere Charles*. Denis' crew take out the herrings until the net is empty and push them below, a process that takes between forty-five minutes and an hour. Denis reckons there are up to 30 tonnes of herring on the *Suzanna G* now. He knows that when they reach Dunmore, both crews will have to work hard to tip the fish from the boats into the big 'bins' on the quayside; each 'bin' can hold a tonne of herrings. The fishery officer will count them, then they will be loaded onto the lorry, which will have to drive onto the weighbridge for a second check before heading off up the quay to a fish factory, maybe in New Ross.

With the third load now tipping into the *Suzanna G*, the *Pere Charles* crew has a bit of respite. Billy O'Connor is already starting to prepare the dinner. It'll take them an hour at least to steam to Dunmore and if they don't get something to eat now, the lads will be cranky.

At 5.00pm Pa Coady chats on his mobile with a friend and says the fishing has been excellent. He doesn't normally talk about his father, but recently he's been talking about him and just like young Simba in *The Lion King*, he says he believes his father is up there somewhere, in the stars.

After the crew of the *Suzanna G* have taken out all the herrings from the net, one of the men on the *Pere Charles* works the lever to take the empty net back onto the *Pere Charles*; the net is wheeled up onto the drum at the stern of the boat. It's 5.15pm. Tom keeps an eye on the operation from his wheelhouse in case both vessels drift too close to each other; if this happens, he gives it a bit of throttle and moves forward a little. But everything goes fine. The net is now back on the drum and secure. Tom reckons it'll probably be 6.30pm or 6.40pm before they are back in Dunmore. Food is the priority now as they have maybe three hard hours of work ahead of them on the quay when they get back. They won't be going out tomorrow as the weather will be bad, but they've had a fantastic catch today and with a bit of luck they'll get out again on Thursday night or early on Friday morning and will finish their quota for the week.

The weather has held up well for them today, though. Denis remarks that it's actually been ideal for herring fishing. But the forecast is bad. It's time to go in.

It's just after 5.15pm and Tom rings Michael Walsh to let him know they are heading for home. Michael Walsh has just left Dunmore and is on his way to take the ferry at Passage East over to Wexford. The weather is freshening, but is not too bad yet. Michael is on top of the world because 'the boys are coming in with a boat full of fish.'

The *Pere Charles* pulls away from the *Suzanna G* and starts heading for Dunmore. The crew of the *Suzanna G* clear off the last few herrings from the deck and put them in the hold. They lock down the manhole cover and give the signal. Denis starts steaming for home as well.

He can see the *Pere Charles* ahead of him and slightly to the right, maybe at a 2 o'clock position. There's only half-a-mile, possibly three-quarters of a mile, between the two boats.

It's 5.40pm and Tom tries to ring Michael to find out about the plans for unloading. Michael has just arrived in home and is on another call when he notices a missed call from Tom's phone. He rings back and he and Tom chat for maybe five minutes.

'Jesus, it's a right auld job when it goes handy,' says Tom.

'What's she like with them?' asks Michael.

Tom tells him that Denis says 'she's like a duck, brilliant, sits lovely, she's grand. We'll get in now and get these things out of her tonight. I'm glad we're booked in for the next week; you could get a couple of handy weeks' wages out of it.'

Alan Caffery from Celtic Seafoods is going to buy the herrings. Michael rings him to say 'the boys are coming in, I think they have about 70 tonne; Tommy has about 50 tonne.'

'Are they landing two boats or one?' asks Alan.

'Jesus, I don't know that. I'll ring him back to ask him.'

*

It's dark now, has been for nearly an hour. It's coming up to 5.50pm. Everything is normal, but the weather is picking up and the 'lump' in the sea is beginning to show. Denis is at the wheel in the *Suzanna G.* His friend and crewmate Brian Crummy has just joined him in the wheelhouse. Suddenly, Tom's voice crackles across on the VHF radio.

'She's broached on me . . . stand by us.'

There is no panic in Tom's voice, but Denis is alarmed. He knows what Tom means. In Denis' experience, when a skipper says his boat has broached, it means it is sideways to the sea and something is happening to it. 'Stand by us' means 'we need you here, now, to keep an eye on us because we could be in trouble'.

Denis starts turning the controls to the right, moving *Suzanna G* towards where he thinks the *Pere Charles* is located.

He's doing 5 knots.

He should be over beside Tom in a few minutes.

With his left hand, he reaches down and moves the knob on the radar, reducing it to the small scale to get rid of the clutter so he can 'get a fix' on the *Pere Charles*. While he's doing this he says to Brian, 'Keep an eye on them'.

Brian takes a few steps forward and moves to the right of the wheelhouse and looks out the window.

It takes no more than two seconds for Denis to get the small radar into position.

He looks around to his right and says to Brian, 'Can you see him?' Brian is straining to see through the darkness. The *Pere*

Charles should be only three-quarters of a mile from where they are.

'I can only see a port light, well . . . I think it's a port light,' says Brian.

'Just keep an eye on it,' says Denis, his mind in overdrive. He looks down to the radar, but for some reason he cannot see the dot that would be the *Pere Charles*. He takes a deep breath, thinking fast. What could be wrong? Why can't he see the boat on the radar? It's less than twenty seconds since Tom said, 'stand by us'. Why can't they see the lights on the boat? Have the lights gone out because of some sort of mechanical failure? If I can't see the boat, Denis thinks, and we're heading over to where it should be, we could end up running into it. He stares hard at the radar again: Why the hell can't I see him? He has to be there.

Denis turns the knob again, to see if he can tune it in better, but he knows this is pointless as it tunes itself automatically.

Suddenly Brian says, 'All I can see is the lights in at Slade. I can't see any port light.'

This cannot be happening. No, it must be there. The port light was there a few seconds ago.

*

Michael Walsh tries to ring Tom to ask him if they are landing fish from both vessels. He can't get him on the phone. Michael doesn't think there's anything strange about this because he reckons Tom is dipping in and out of coverage. He tries again, but still can't get through. He rings Denis' phone, but it's engaged; Michael thinks Denis and Tom are talking. He'll give them a few minutes and then ring back.

*

Denis grips the controls tighter. He's now brought the *Suzanna G* as close as possible to where he thinks the *Pere Charles* should be.

Neither he nor Brian can see any lights.

There is absolutely no sign of the *Pere Charles*.

'Where are you Tom?' Denis thinks in silent desperation. 'You must be here.'

Denis eases back on the throttle and stops the *Suzanna G*, knocking it out of gear. He doesn't want to run into the *Pere Charles* in the darkness. Denis has all his lights on. He looks out the window, every direction. Still, nothing. A dart of panic shoots through him. He turns to the VHF radio and picks up the speaker.

'*Pere Charles*, we can't see you, Tom. Tom, are you there? Tom? Come in Tom?'

No answer. He tries again.

'Tom, come in Tom, this is Denis here.'

Denis and Brian are now extremely worried. Why isn't he responding? Is there something wrong with the VHF? Try him on the mobile phone. Quickly. They're close enough to shore and Denis has a full signal on his phone. He hits redial; the last person he spoke to was Tom.

Denis waits. 'Please, Tom, please be there, answer the phone.' Nothing. Then a woman's voice: 'The Vodafone customer you are calling is not accessible at the moment or may have their mobile powered off. Please try again later.'

Denis and Brian look at one another. They know something is very wrong. There's no way Tom would turn off his mobile phone. They strain into the darkness for any sign of anything, any movement, any shape. All the *Suzanna*'s lights are on, if the boat is

80

there, he'll see it. If the boat is floating, he'll see it. If there is anybody in the water with any sort of reflective gear, he'll see them.

Black darkness is all they can see. Nothing else. There is no sign of anything on, or in the water. They start shouting, calling out the names. The rising wind swallows their cries. Denis races to the VHF, turns the dial and is straight through to the Marine Rescue Coordination Centre in Dublin.

'This is the fishing trawler the *Suzanna G*, I think we have a problem with the *Pere Charles*. It's gone off the radar. The last known location is two-and-a-half miles south of Hook Head. We weren't far . . .'

*

Less than 20 miles west of the *Pere Charles*' last-known position, the *Honey Dew II* is bracing itself against the weather.

Ger, Tomasz, Viktor and Vladimir have been fishing since early afternoon. They left Kinsale at 6.20am that morning. The catch has been very poor.

News comes through on the radio that a boat has gone down off Dunmore. Ger knows the boat. He talks on the VHF to his friend Johnny, who is around 25 miles south-east of him in the *Rachel Jay*. They have spoken a few times during the day and have also emailed each other from their lap-tops when out of coverage. They discuss what they've heard about Dunmore and say how terrible it is, and hope they crew will be found alive. They also talk about the worsening weather; they say they'll fish away and see how it goes.

Ger tells Tomasz, Vladimir and Viktor about the *Pere Charles* and says he asked if they needed help over there, but was told there were enough boats helping.

The winds along the south coast at 9.00pm are strong, ranging from 35 knots to 40 knots. A gale warning has been given and the weather has been deteriorating since before 6.00pm. The south-westerly winds are blowing up the 'left-over waves' from the previous day and by 10.00pm it's gusting 43 knots over a heavy sea. Storm Force 10 winds are approaching.

As soon as the wind starts increasing in strength (from around 5.00pm), it immediately increases the height and power of the waves. The particular feature about this storm is that the wind has accelerated at an enormous rate over a short period of time, with gusts of 22 knots rising to 52 knots within just six hours. This is a phenomenon that weather forecasters don't see too often on Irish coasts. The water temperature is 10° Celsius, which gives a survival time of two hours for a person wearing 'normal' clothes (not survival suits), if he's able to stay afloat.

*

A few miles to the south of the *Honey Dew* is the Marathon oil and gas platform. The weather-reading equipment there is 30m (98ft) up from the surface of the sea and it records information every fifteen minutes. By 9.00pm it is recording winds of 50 knots, but by 1.00am the gusts have reached 67 knots, then 69, and continue to gust at this strength until 4.00am when they start decreasing, but only slowly. The weather isn't just bad where the *Honey Dew* is, it is horrendous.

Vladimir and Viktor have both been out in big storms before, but this is one of the worst they have ever seen. The nets are hauled in just after 8.00pm, with Tomasz working one side and Vladimir and Viktor the other. Tomasz is tall and strong; the other two small and wiry, all three are tough and hardened. The catch is again not good and working conditions on deck are now very difficult. Ger decides they'll stop fishing because the weather is so bad and will move closer to land until the storm blows itself out. They'll resume fishing in the morning, if things improve. Tomasz goes into the galley and prepares some chicken fillets for dinner. Ger stays in the wheelhouse while the others eat, and when Viktor is finished he takes over while Ger tucks into Tomasz's excellent cooking. By 9.00pm the weather is deteriorating rapidly and the waves are getting bigger and bigger. The *Honey Dew* is now 'dodging into the weather', moving the boat into the oncoming wind and waves with just enough power to literally 'ride out the storm'. After Ger finishes his meal, he asks Viktor to check on the pumps and other gear in the engine room to make sure everything is okay. Viktor has a diploma in engineering and knows the engine in the *Honey Dew* is in great working condition. He checks everything and all is functioning perfectly.

*

Mary Bohan is upstairs at home, putting the three youngest children to bed when Ger phones. It's just after 9.00pm. She puts the phone on loud speaker and they all say hello and chat to him.

At the end Ger says, 'Goodnight all and say your prayers.'

He tells Mary he'll talk to her later.

Mary knows it's a wild night but has no great concern.

By 11.30pm, with the weather a lot worse, she phones him.

'How are things?' she says.

'Grand hon,' he responds.

'Where are you?' says Mary.

'I'm in the boat,' says Ger, his usual humour to the fore.

'I know! But where's the boat?'

'In the water!' says Ger, laughing.

He tells her how many miles off they are and they chat for a few minutes.

Ger says it's a tough night and they are battening down after having had their food.

They say goodnight and that they love each other.

Mary tries to get some sleep, but this is the first night she's ever worried about Ger being out. She had heard the news earlier about the sinking of the *Pere Charles* and this is on her mind. Outside her window, the wind is screeching non-stop.

Less than a mile away, Aneta cannot sleep either.

She looks out of the window a number of times and shudders to see how bad the weather is. She tries calling Tomasz a number of times but can't get him as they are now out of mobile phone range. She sends a text message to her friends saying that she is scared. She hardly sleeps. Instead, she prays for the safe return of her husband.

Meanwhile, the 712-tonne Irish Naval Vessel, the *Le Orla*, is heading back to base at Haulbawline in Cork. It had been going towards Dunmore East to assist in the search for the *Pere Charles* and for possible survivors. But as it passed the coastline from Ballycotton, such was the strength of the waves and wind that it rolled 45 degrees. The captain has decided it is too dangerous to continue and is heading back to port.

*

Just before midnight, Johnny and Ger talk on the VHF. They chat about different things for twenty minutes. Ger says their catch wasn't good and that he's 6 miles east of Minehead, off west Waterford. Johnny is 25 miles south-east, further out into the

Celtic Sea. Ger is in good form, but says he's not going to fish any more tonight due to the bad weather. He complains: 'Seventy litres an hour just to make headway and we're only doing three-and-a-half knots.'

Ger says he's going to head a bit closer to the coast and if the weather isn't any better in the morning, he'll go back to Kinsale. Johnny suggests that Ger should head for Dunmore, but Ger doesn't really like going into Dunmore because it's not that sheltered and his boat is quite big (22m/72ft). He says he would go into Ballycotton only for the fact that they're doing up the harbour and he says he can't get in there.

'Well, boy, are you hauling now or are you leaving it till one, will you make up your mind?' he says to Johnny.

Johnny isn't due to haul his nets until 1.00am, but because of the weather he might do it half-an-hour earlier. Ger wants to know because he will stay up and see what sort of a haul Johnny gets; if he's not hauling until 1.00am, then he'll turn in for the night. In the end, Johnny says he doesn't know.

At midnight Met Eireann issues a warning of potentially the strongest weather in what has been a stormy winter. Gale Force 8 to storm Force 10 winds are predicted, with severe gusts and the possibility of reaching violent storm Force 11. Winds are now gusting up to 57 knots and wave heights are 7.2m (23ft) or more in places.

Around fifteen minutes after he has spoken to Ger, Johnny decides to haul up the net. It's now coming up to 12.30am. Ger decides to climb into his bunk beside the wheelhouse as he's been up since before 6.00am this morning; Tomasz and Viktor go down to their bunks below deck to see if they can get some sleep. Vladimir stays on watch in the wheelhouse; he will wake them if

there is a problem or if he gets tired. Ger has told him to continue 'dodging' into the weather.

Around 1.00am Johnny radios Ger to tell him he has hauled. When he receives no reply, he presumes that Ger has gone to his bunk. He knows the other crew members normally wouldn't answer the VHF for a call such as this.

At this stage, there are only six boats off the entire southern coast of Ireland: the *Honey Dew*, the *Rachel Jay*, a French trawler 10 miles from the *Rachel Jay*, and three other vessels. The waves pound the boats incessantly and the awesome seas continue to swell in size.

Some of the waves that hit the *Honey Dew* send water over the highest point of the boat. Every few seconds the boat crashes down into the troughs left behind by these monsters. But every time, it comes back up and ploughs into, up, over or through the next wave. But there is no let-up, not for a moment, on and on they come, some bigger than others, some more violent, some more destructive. But the *Honey Dew's* engine drives it on without fail; Vladimir later says that at no time did the engine cause problems.

He thinks the weather can't get any worse, but by 3.00am it's more ferocious, more terrifying than it has been all night. He reckons it must be Force 10, possibly stronger. He has never seen anything like this.

Vladimir feels his battle with the elements is not going well and reckons some of the waves must be at least 14m (44ft) high. The boat is taking a terrible pounding. Some of the waves are breaking down on top of it: the weight of water from a 14m high wave being pushed by 60 knot winds is akin to landing a massive boulder or series of boulders on the wooden deck. How the *Honey Dew* can withstand it is testimony to how well the boat was built. But all it may take is one or more massive waves to wreak some serious damage. Sea spray and rain lashes the windows of the wheelhouse, making visibility very poor. Vladimir has no idea how big the next wave is going to be. The winds hit a horrifying 66 knots.

Just after 3.00am a series of waves crashes down on the vessel with such ferocity that Vladimir feels he needs to wake Ger. He goes to Ger's bunk and calls him. Ger gets up, has a look at everything and tells Vladimir to get some sleep, that he'll take over the watch. Vladimir turns to go down the steps to the bunk. Just as he turns, they are hit by a massive, awful, stomach-churning bang. Vladimir feels it must be an enormous wave, a wall of water. He is thrown violently to the side. He tries to stand up, but the *Honey Dew* has already started listing to the port side. He knows the normal motion of the *Honey Dew*, how it leans over, then rights itself, that back-and-forth rhythm, but this time, it feels different.

Another wave hits, and another . . . pounding . . . pounding . . . pounding.

Something has gone terribly wrong. Maybe the sheer force of water has split open some of the timbers; maybe water is flooding in below-deck; maybe the waves have caused structural damage to the hull and water is gushing in there. Could something else have hit the boat, like a container? The boat falls over farther, then takes another juddering hit. The boat's timbers creak and groan under the pressure. She's not going to make it.

Ger shouts to Vladimir to get Viktor and Tomasz up immediately. Vladimir can hardly stand up; everything is shifting to the side; Ger is holding onto the controls, trying to bring his beloved boat back from the brink. Not only is it listing drastically to the port side, it is now being pushed around and can no longer drive up through the waves. They are fast reaching the sickening point of no return.

The boat is now broadside to the mighty sea and the power of the waves is fearsome. Another monster smashes down on the deck, more water gushes in. Ger is finding it hard to stand. He's a big, strong man, but the whites on his knuckles are showing and every muscle is tensed as he tries desperately to hold onto the controls.

Vladimir somehow makes it to the second top step on the way to the bunks and roars for the men, who are already getting up; they come up just as the water starts flooding in.

They can feel the boat going over and over, around and around, slowly at first, but now gathering speed. Vladimir reckons it's taken only around thirty seconds to reach this point of devastation.

The wheelhouse door is on the starboard side. The men have to roar to hear each other, such is the noise from the wind and the waves. Ger shouts for them to get the life-rafts. He takes the radio and shouts: 'May Day, May Day – this is the *Honey Dew II*, help, help, we are in trouble, we're sinking, May Day, May Day. . .'

The wheelhouse is starting to fill with water. Tomasz manages to push open the door and pull himself out. Vladimir follows. Just outside the door, on the left, is a life-raft inside a container and beside it hangs a life-ring. Viktor stays with Ger in the wheelhouse. Everything is happening very quickly and the noise is overwhelming: the waves roaring, pounding and grinding; the wind howling and screeching. Ger shouts for Viktor to get out.

Ger calls again on the VHF for help, but the boat is now nearly fully over. The lights are still working, but for how long? Ger grabs the radio again and shouts, 'MAY DAY, MAY DAY'.

No response.

The waves must have ripped the antennae off the roof. He tries again.

'MAY DAY, MAY DAY.'

Nothing.

He lifts the flap on the red distress button and presses it. This should send out an immediate distress signal on what is known as the DSC VHF, which the *Rachel Jay* and other boats should hear. But Ger knows that if he's not getting any response on the radio, his communications with the outside world may be non-existent. The terrifying reality hits as another wave slams. Viktor roars at Ger to leave the radio and come outside, but Ger knows it's his job as skipper to get a message to someone that they're going down. And he doesn't know if they will survive the ferocious storm outside.

Viktor goes to help Vladimir and Tomasz. He glances back through the wheelhouse window. He sees Ger isn't panicking, that he's calling out again in the hope someone will answer his distress call. He puts his head in the door again and shouts for Ger to come on. The *Honey Dew* is now nearly completely over as another wave hits. Ger tries again and waits for somebody to respond. He knows that if he doesn't get a May Day call out, nobody will know where they are. Everything is working against him – the silent radio, the force of gravity, the water nearly up to his waist.

Suddenly, the water blows out the windows in the wheelhouse.

Ger seems to be pressed up against the wall of the wheelhouse by the force of the water. He's still holding onto the radio.

Tomasz has managed to open the life-raft; it inflates instantly; they throw it into the sea while somehow holding onto its rope.

It's only a matter of seconds before the *Honey Dew* will turn over completely.

Tomasz tries pulling the life-raft closer to the vessel; the rope is wet and slippery.

Then, the lights go out.

More windows start cracking and blowing out.

The engine stops.

Disorientation . . . noise . . . water . . . panic . . . fear . . . cold . . . shock . . . terror . . .

And then, the crucial moment. The boat goes over.

There is water everywhere.

The three men try to jump up and out. They have not managed to get lifejackets on.

The suction is immense as the water and the boat try to pull them down.

If they get trapped under the boat, they're gone . . . there's utter confusion.

Viktor thinks he can see Tomasz trying to hold onto the rope of the life-raft and thinks he has the life-ring, which he grabbed just as they went over. Nobody knows if Ger has managed to get out of the wheelhouse. Viktor is certain he was still in the wheelhouse as the boat turned over.

The wheelhouse would have filled with water very quickly. Ger may have tried to escape through one of the windows, or the door, but the force of water may have pushed him back. It would have been completely dark, everything upside-down and confusing.

Ger is alone. The water is cold, but not paralysing. As the water rises, the roar of the waves fades away. Maybe he is knocked unconscious, or maybe he takes one last gulp of air as the water reaches his chin. If this happens, he would close his eyes and hold his breath for as long as possible, anything from 30 seconds to a minute probably. In this scenario, he would now be completely submerged and all manner of thoughts would race through this mind. If he can't get out, his body may assume a certain peacefulness. There would be only a few more seconds before he cannot hold his breath any longer. And then it's over.

Outside, Tomasz, Viktor and Vladimir are all sucked under the water; they hold their breaths; the terrible coldness of the water shocks their bodies; their eyes are closed involuntarily as they kick and kick and scramble and kick ... the water pushes them up . . . flings them to the side . . . sucks them down again . . . they gulp air and water . . . and kick and scramble again . . . the sound on the surface is unbelievable . . . the sound underwater is muffled and it is dark, pitch dark . . .

Viktor manages to reach the surface. His clothes are heavy, he knows he doesn't have long. He looks around, desperately scanning the water for any sign of life.

Darkness.

He descends into the trough of a 10m (32ft) wave.

He thinks he sees the small light on the life-ring; it must be Tomasz.

He kicks with all his might and begins rising on the next wave, but the water breaks over him.

He gets his head out above water once more and gulps air desperately.

He thinks he can see Vladimir clinging to the bottom of the now upturned boat.

Suddenly, he sees the small light again. He swims towards it. Yes, it is Tomasz. They roar at each other that they are okay.

Then, maybe 5m (16–22ft) away, they see another small light ...

it must be the light on the top of the life-raft . . . they have to get to it . . . it's their only hope . . . their final chance.

Viktor flaps and kicks and scrambles and gulps . . . it's not his moment to die, not yet . . . and the sea agrees, sending a wave to carry him towards the life-raft.

Tomasz is behind him, swimming as hard as he can. He reaches the life-raft first. It hasn't fully inflated.

Viktor reaches the life-raft just as another huge wave hits.

Tomasz is thrown back, away.

Viktor is thrown at least 4m (13ft) from the life-raft.

Everything is happening so quickly and it's all so disorienting.

Meanwhile, Vladimir has managed to keep his head up above the water and for a split-second, beside the upturned hull of the *Honey Dew*, he thinks he can see the silhouette of two people near what looks like the life-raft.

The boat is now completely upside-down and rapidly filling with water. The stern seems to be filling quicker and it looks like it's going to sink stern-first.

Vladimir is struggling against the churning water, then another massive wave hits. The power is so almighty, it pushes Tomasz further away.

Viktor is on the other side and goes under the water again. When he finally manages to resurface, he can't see Tomasz anywhere.

Vladimir gets his head above the water and is immediately overwhelmed by the next wave, but mercifully it pushes him towards the life-raft, which he can suddenly see with its small light. He knows if he doesn't go for it immediately, he may not get another chance.

He summons up every ounce of strength he has left in his thin body and strikes out towards it. Another wave is just about to push it away, but with one massive effort, he reaches out and grabs it.

A few seconds ago, he thought he saw the outline of two people close to it, but now, nobody is there.

He holds onto the rope that runs along the outside of the life-raft and begins shouting the names of his crewmates, his friends. Vladimir knows that only one life-raft has been released; they didn't have time to launch the other one.

Less than 30m (98ft) away, the *Honey Dew* is about to disappear. The last remaining visible section of the hull is sucked under and with that, the *Honey Dew II* is gone from sight. The EPRIB doesn't go off – it must have been trapped under the vessel in such a way that it cannot float free. It goes down, down, down with the boat. Its signal will never be activated. Does anybody apart from the three men know the boat is gone?

Viktor has been fighting frantically to stay afloat as the sea has struggled equally hard to pull him down; his clothes feel like lead weights; but there now, again, is the life-raft. He hasn't much energy left, but he must get to it, he has to get to it. He's wearing three jumpers, two pairs of trousers and heavy shoes – everything is wet and every bone in his body wants to stop and rest, but the mind is not ready to give up. Something inside him tells him to survive.

With herculean effort he swims the last few metres to the life-raft. Visibility is down to less than 2m (6ft). On the other side of it, Vladimir is just climbing inside. Vladimir is shouting the names of the others, then suddenly, below him in the water, is his lifelong friend. He pulls Viktor into the small raft beside him. Neither man can believe what has happened. Neither man can believe he is actually in the life-raft. Neither man can believe he is alive. Viktor asks Vladimir where Tomasz is, but he says he doesn't know.

There is a lot of water in the life-raft, but it's staying afloat. The two are nearly oblivious to it as they shout and roar the names of their missing colleagues.

'GER! TOMASZ! GER! TOMASZ!'

They scan the water for the light on the life-ring, hoping to spot it and, with it, Tomasz. But there is nothing other than water – dark, cold, menacing water.

Vladimir and Viktor cling to the ropes in the life-raft. They have to stand in the raft as there is so much water in it, nearly up to their waist. They rise up on each wave and are thrown awkwardly to the side. They come down from each steep height at speed. It's still pitch black. Crest and trough, crest and trough, the movement of the little raft on that swollen, raging sea is violent and sickening. They are being flung through the cascading water, every moment another miracle to be alive at all. They search in one of the compartments the life-raft and find a whistle. They take turns blowing it as hard as they can.

No reply. No voices shouting, no sign of any movement in the water.

It starts to rain hard, really hard.

Both men have had life-raft training, so they know this raft can hold six people. It is only 2m x 1m. It is bright orange and has a canopy on it. It is very difficult, nearly impossible, to stand up in one of these rafts. If you do, you risk falling out. But Viktor and Vladimir have no option as there is so much water in it. With every wave, the two are terrified it will be turned over, but it doesn't. Somehow, it stays upright. They hold on for dear life as the waves pummel them from every side and the noise of the storm deafens them.

Viktor is still sure they are going to see Tomasz because he is certain he saw him with the life-ring.

The minutes tick by. They have no real sense of how long they have been calling, but they feel their legs, which are partially submerged in water, getting colder and colder. Their bodies are saturated, the rain is beating into their faces – it's like standing in a power shower for ten minutes and not being allowed to look away from the water source. Twenty seconds would be painful; imagine trying to do it for ten minutes.

They know from their military training and knowledge of the sea that the biggest threat at this stage is hypothermia. They know that taking off their wet clothes will not increase their body temperatures. They need to zip up the canopy to prevent any more cold water getting in, but they are not going to do that until they find Ger and Tomasz.

The minutes pass, and so too does hope. After about an hour they are exhausted from shouting and searching. The boat is gone, there is no sign of anything in the water, man or man-made, no life-rings, no Tomasz, no Ger. Vladimir and Viktor are alone in a raging storm, on a small inflatable raft, facing high seas the like of which these seasoned fishermen have never seen before. For now they are alive, but is survival possible?

*

Thirty miles away, Johnny Walsh has been dodging the *Rachel Jay* into the dreadful weather since he hauled in the nets. He goes to bed around 4.00am and Michael O'Donovan takes over the night-watch until 10.00am. They have no idea that the *Honey Dew II* and its crew, their friends, have been involved in a catastrophic event. No one knows that the *Honey Dew* has sunk. No one knows that two men are crouched low and shivering in a life-raft, fighting for their lives. And that means, no one is coming to help them.

*

Vladimir and Viktor realise the life-raft is filling with water, both from the rain and from the crashing waves. They know it should have been zipped shut from the moment they got into it. Now, the cold and fear of hypothermia is overwhelming, but they still don't want to zip up the canopy because of what that gesture will mean.

They once again search the compartments tucked into the fabric of the raft. They find a small plastic cup and start bailing out the water.

They also locate the two small packets containing plastic, all-in-one bodysuits known as a Thermal Protective Aids. They remember that they shouldn't remove their wet clothes yet, and instead put on the bodysuits over their clothes. This prevents them losing body heat and makes them feel warmer. In a while they might take off the wet clothes and try to dry them, but that is going to be very difficult. They find sachets containing 50mls of water. They drink a few of them, keeping the water in their mouths for a while before swallowing so as to keep their mouths moist.

The raft's compartments also hold some specially constituted carbohydrate biscuits. Experts reckon that to sustain energy, a person needs 0.5 litres of water and 3,000KJs of food everyday. Those energy requirements are provided by these long-life biscuits, which come in small slabs. Vladimir and Viktor break off a 3-inch biscuit each and eat it. They will need only three of these over a twenty-four-hour period to maintain their energy levels. They eat a few of them because they are very hungry and weak.

It seems like they've been in the life-raft for hours. They are cold, wet, frightened and very sad. Eventually, the moment comes when they have to admit that there's no hope of finding Ger or

Tomasz. They can see or hear nothing, and they feel the waves have pushed them further away from where they think the boat sank. With heavy hearts, they reluctantly pull up the zip on the life-raft and close it over them to stop the water getting in. Up to now, they have been calling out the names of the missing men constantly. They now believe they won't see them alive again. There's nothing for it but to ride out the storm as best they can. It's a terrible moment for the two survivors.

In those desperate hours, thoughts swirl around in their minds. Viktor thinks of his daughter and son, Viktoria and Dima. He thinks of why he came to Ireland four years ago, of how he came to Kinsale. The only time he had been outside of Lithuania before that was when he was in the army and went on a training operation to Russia. He likes Ireland, but finds it very difficult to be away from his wife and children. He wants to see them now. The last time he was home was five months ago, when he brought Vladimir with him back to Ireland. They've been friends for many years.

Vladimir has one daughter, Skyeesta, whom he misses terribly. He thinks about his days and years fishing, all the different countries he has fished from, including that time when he was fishing off Iceland and saw a boat sink. He had just finished a contract on the boat and had gone over to fish from another when the first one sank. It wasn't his time then and, so far, this is not his time either.

The men are shivering. They have bailed out as much water as they can. They look through every inch of the raft to see what might help them. There's some medical equipment and tablets. Neither of them is physically injured, but both have awful headaches. Vladimir feels sickly and thinks it's because he swallowed water and oil when he was in the water. They take the tablets, hoping their stomachs will settle. They are sea-sickness tablets, which are provided in every life-raft because one of the main causes of death at this stage could be hypovolemia. If somebody is being thrown about in a raft, they may suffer terrible and continuous sea-sickness. If they vomit continuously, they lose vital fluids, which can lead to hypvolemic shock, causing the organs to shut down.

The two men tuck their feet in under their bodies and face each other. They talk about what has happened, about their wives and their children, about life. They both think they were hit by a massive, possibly a 'freak' wave, which Viktor thinks broke the timbers. They try to talk about as many things as possible. They are very tired, but they don't want to fall asleep in case they miss the rescue helicopter. They resolve not to give in.

After what seems like many more hours, Vladimir and Viktor notice that it's not as dark anymore. They open the life-raft and see that dawn is creeping slowly across the horizon. The waves are abating a little, but Vladimir reckons it's probably still Force 7. They guess it might be around 8.00am. With the daylight comes renewed hope that they are going to be rescued. Yes, they definitely think they will be rescued. They set off some flares in the hope that a fishing boat or helicopter may be nearby. Perhaps Ger did get out that frantic May Day call, perhaps someone heard and has alerted the authorities. Surely soon, someone will come searching for them?

PART III

SEARCH AND RESCUE

8

Abandoning the Safety of Shore

Jim Griffin has been on his knees all day, laying wooden floors. He arrives home in Dunmore at around 5.25pm and chats with his wife, Caroline, and their three girls as they prepare dinner. Joan Bowe is at home in Grantstown, in the city, getting the dinner ready with her husband, Christy. Jim is the Area Officer for the Irish Coast Guard in Dunmore; Joan is Deputy Area Officer. Both joined the Coast Guard service seven years ago to help the community and, in particular, to help people in trouble. For Jim, the decision to join up came after he lost one of his best friends to the sea. Peter Nolan drowned on the *Jenalisa*, and after that, Jim felt he had to help save others from drowning, and from grieving.

Just before 6.00pm a fisherman rings Jim saying a boat might be in trouble. Jim heads down to the Coast Guard station. The wind is so strong he has difficulty opening the door of his van to get inside. It's only half-an-hour since he arrived home; he has never seen the wind pick up so much strength so quickly. 'God help the men out there if a boat is in trouble,' he thinks grimly.

Joan has heard 'some commotion' on her VHF in the kitchen and, given the ferocity of the weather, alarm bells start ringing in her mind. She phones Jim, but just then her bleep goes off. It's a message from the Marine Rescue Coordination Centre (MRCC) in Dublin to all eighteen members of the Dunmore East Coast Guard: that's their signal to get to the station as quickly as possible. It's an emergency.

Richard Byrne, Gordan Duncan and Paul Breivik are working their shift in MRCC in Leeson Lane, in Dublin. It's a big room stacked with computers, buttons and charts. They are all full-time members of the Irish Coast Guard, which is run with military-like precision.

It's only a few seconds since Paul received a call from Denis Harding, the skipper of the *Suzanna G*, that the *Pere Charles* had gone off the radar. Denis had spoken on Channel 16 of his VHF from his boat directly to MRCC. And now, further confirmation that something is seriously wrong – the EPIRB on the *Pere Charles* has been activated.

As the vessel sank, the hydrostatic release was activated and it cut the EPIRB away from the doomed vessel. The released EPIRB has now bobbed back to the surface and started transmitting its unique signal. This signal is picked up by one of two satellites – one Russian, one American – which cover the North Atlantic. The signal is sent automatically to a central command in Lamest, in south-east England, from where it's relayed straight to Kinloss in Scotland, where UK Coast Guard officials see it come up on the screen.

It's 6.02pm; the phone rings in MRCC in Dublin. 'Kinloss here, we've received an EPIRB report on Irish Fishing Vessel, *Pere Charles*.'

Breivik immediately telephones the Coast Guard Search and Rescue (SAR) helicopter centre in Waterford Regional Airport. Kilmore Quay and Dunmore East lifeboats are bleeped. A full-scale search-and-rescue mission for the *Pere Charles* is now underway.

Most of the senior Coast Guard officers are still at HQ. They stay behind to assist in whatever way they can. It's decided that one senior officer, Ger Hegarty, will drive to Dunmore immediately to set up an incident room.

At the time, Geoff Livingstone is Chief of the Coast Guard and Norman Fullam is his Deputy. They know that the Irish Coast Guard is very fortunate in the numbers of people, both volunteers and professionals, it can call on at times like this. 'I think it comes from the fact that the weather is traditionally so bad here and that the sea has taken so many people,' says Fullam, who was involved in 1995 in the search for the six men missing off Donegal when the *Carrickatine* sank. 'There's a great tradition of responding to people in trouble.'

Captain Peter McKenzie Brown is on duty at SAR in Waterford Airport. The dedicated MRCC 'scramble' phone rings at 6.04pm and all the details are relayed.

The crew of four put on their orange Gortex immersion suits. Co-pilot Mike Farquhar goes out with winchman Brodie Prideaux to start up the helicopter with the engineers. Peter and winch-operator John Manning plan the mission. Met Eireann advises them of the weather they will be going up into; extra fuel will be needed.

By 6.18pm the SAR helicopter is airborne.

Neville Murphy is at home, looking forward to a quiet night in when his bleeper suddenly goes off: 'ALB LAUNCH'. It's a call for the launch of the All Weather Lifeboat. He grabs his jacket and heads out into one of the worst nights he's ever seen. And Neville has seen many bad nights: he's a winchman with SAR in Waterford and in his spare time, is a volunteer for the RNLI at Dunmore.

The crew of seven arrives at the lifeboat station and are told that the *Pere Charles* is missing. Each of them knows at least one of the men on board. They get into their gear as quickly as possible. Ray Power is coxswain. John Glody and his younger brother, Pat, are there, as is David Murphy, son of Joefy (who is number one coxswain, but is unwell and can't go out). There is also Aidan Kearns, son of the ex-station mechanic. Everybody has a job to do. They all know their drills. Peter Curran is the full-time mechanic with the RNLI in Dunmore. He revs up the engine; others start letting go of the ropes; Neville sits in front of the GPS plotter; Ray is upstairs in the bridge, driving the boat. They head out at speed into the driving wind and rain. The time is 6.23pm.

*

At 6.10pm Michael Walsh finally gets through to Denis on his mobile phone.

'Denis, I've been trying to get you, are you landing one boat or two boats?'

'I'll be back to you in a minute, there's a problem with Tom,' says Denis.

'What do you mean, a problem?'

'He's gone off the radar for the last few minutes.'

'Jesus, ring me when you know anything.'

Michael puts down the phone; he knows in his heart the boat is gone.

He turns around to his wife, Bernie, and says, 'The boat is gone; I'll be back later when I see what's happening,' then rushes out to the car.

Alan Caffery, the fish buyer, rings him a few minutes later to ask how many trucks are needed.

'What's the story, Michael?'

'The boat is gone. Fuck the boat, I'm only interested in the lads now,' says Michael.

He drives towards Dunmore, praying all the way that the lads had time to get into a life-raft. The next few hours will be crucial, but he's hopeful they are going to be found.

*

Lulu finishes work and goes to her Mum's to collect Christine and Jane. Her sister Jenny and brother-in-law Lee are there because Lee is waiting for the *Pere Charles* to dock; he's going to help Tom unload the herrings. Lulu leaves to take the girls home. Lee says he'll go down to the quay to meet the boat as it comes in. Just then, his phone rings. It's a friend of his, a fisherman.

'Oh, that's great,' says his friend, sounding relieved.

'What do you mean?' asks Lee.

'You answered your phone, like, it can't be too bad.'

'What are you on about?'

Lee's friend has been listening to the VHF and thought Lee was on the *Pere Charles*. He tells him what he's heard. Lee can't believe it. Shaking, he tells Jenny, who immediately rings Lulu.

Lulu is at home with the girls, making dinner, looking forward to seeing Tom. Her phone rings. It's Jenny.

'Lu, there's something wrong with Tom's boat.'

'What do you mean?'

'It's gone off the radar. We want you to come down here.'

Lulu is shaking with fear; she's finding it hard to breathe. She doesn't want to alarm the girls. She rings Cathy, her next-door neighbour, who agrees to look after the girls for the night, if necessary; Cathy's husband drives Lulu straight down to the lifeboat station. Jenny and their father, John, are standing up at the harbour wall, looking out. They come down when they see Lulu and the three of them go over to the lifeboat station. The lifeboat has just gone out.

*

Rescue Helicopter 117 begins climbing to 304m (1,000ft). The Sikorsky S61N is a big, old air frame, but is considered ideal for search-and-rescue because it's sturdy, strong and handles extremely well in bad conditions. A mile out from the airport, Peter asks Mike to tune one of their two 'homer' radios to a specific frequency. The second he does this, the EPIRB signal is picked up. They head for it.

Peter normally flies at the cruising speed of 120 knots (118mph), but tonight it's not possible because the wind is so strong. From his seat, the winchman operates a camera called a 'FLIR' (Forward Looking Infra Red), which is attached to the undercarriage. It can turn 360° inside its casing. Brodie flicks a switch and the camera is now in infra-red mode – the only way to see through this darkness.

Within four minutes of take-off, Rescue 117 descends to 60m (200ft), i.e. normal operating height. They fly over where they think the EPIRB is in the water and get what's known as a 'code of silence', in other words the instant they fly over the EPIRB, the signal distorts or crackles a bit, which confirms its exact location. At the same moment they flick another switch on the autopilot system. This will take the helicopter round in an arc and bring them right back to the now marked EPIRB position, where it will hold them in a hover position 100 yards or so from the device. They direct the spotlight down into the water and Brodie scans the monitor of his FLIR. They are expecting to see at least one person in the water, possibly a man holding onto the EPIRB.

Below, they can see the EPIRB. There's nobody with it or near it. It's 6.24pm.

A few seconds later, they spot an orange Calor gas bottle and a life-ring. But again, there's nobody to be seen, apart from the men on the *Suzanna G*, nearby scanning the surface.

'At this point, it's very depressing,' says Peter. 'People's heads are always above the surface. They can be spotted very easily by the FLIR camera as the water temperature is around 10° Celcius and body and head temperature is 38° Celcius. So if there was anybody there, we would have found them.'

They radio MRCC and report the life-ring and gas bottle.

Normally, when a boat sinks, there can be a lot of oil rising to the surface and debris. In the area around the EPIRB, nothing.

They do what is known as a 'clover-leaf search', using the EPIRB as the centre, or 'hot spot', and working out from there in sweeping arcs of 1 mile to cover the immediate area, where survivors are most likely to be in the water.

Nothing.

The crew simply cannot believe it. They fully expected to find the men.

*

The weather has deteriorated still further, and now the night is a maelstrom of wind and driving rain, with the winds hitting Force 10. The brave men and women on the lifeboat put their faces into the wind and focus on their destination. The log book in the station will describe it as 'a very filthy night'.

The seas are heavy and getting worse. The lifeboat is lurching up and down on very big waves, some 7m (23ft) high. The lifeboat can only do 18 knots in these seas (normally it can reach 25).

The lifeboat arrives on scene at 6.38pm. The *Suzanna G* is there and the helicopter is overhead, but there is nothing else to see, only monstrous waves. The lifeboat has a searchlight that can normally penetrate 200 yards, but tonight visibility is very limited.

The crew in the Sikorsky helicopter gives the lifeboat crew the coordinates of the EPIRB and the lifeboat heads for that. Within five minutes they spot the flashing EPIRB light and recover it from the water. Then they get the life-ring and the gas cylinder. The crew uses binoculars and night-vision goggles in an attempt to find survivors, but there is nothing. The weather means the searchlight is about as useful as headlights in thick fog – all they are seeing is horizontal spray. Peter Curran says he has never seen as bad a night, never seen water and wind combined so violently. Nonetheless, they keep at it, ignoring the waves that seem intent on toppling them and scanning the water for anything, any sign. Above them, the Sikorsky goes up and down, covering miles of sea as it searches and searches.

*

In Kerry, Pat Frank and his brother, Dan, have just come home after their day's work landscape gardening. Both are sitting in their work clothes in Pat Frank's sitting room, watching the 6.00 news on RTÉ 1. Just before 6.45pm, newsreader Bryan Dobson reports that a fishing trawler is missing out of Dunmore East; no name is given.

Pat's heart sinks. At that moment, for whatever reason, he just knows. Dan knows, too.

'Jesus Christ, that's Tomaisín,' says Dan.

Pat tries to calm him. 'Ah, it's not,' he says, 'that *craic* is happening the whole time, like, you know. Sure, whoever it is would be in the rafts anyway if they got them out.'

Pat picks up his mobile and rings Tom's number.

'The Vodafone customer you are trying to call may have . . .'

He tells Dan, who goes straight up to their parents' house. Julia, Tom's mother, rings Lulu in Dunmore.

'Lu, did you hear about the boat off Dunmore? Do you know who it is?' asks Julia.

Lulu hesitates. 'Julia, it's your son.'

With that, Lulu breaks down and cries, heaving sobs of fear and grief. She won't ever remember the rest of the conversation.

Julia is shaking as she turns to her family and says, 'It's them alright.'

Pat Frank and Dan decide to leave immediately. They jump into Pat's car, work clothes and boots still on. They're going to drive straight to Dunmore, no stopping, a four-hour drive that will be brutal – the worst journey either man will ever make. Pat Frank rings Lulu, tries to calm her down, tells her he knows how the boats work and that 'If Tom had a chance to send a mayday, that was good. If he had time to do that, he'd have time to get the lads onto the life-raft.'

That calms Lulu somewhat, but a few minutes later somebody

tells her the mayday wasn't issued by Tom; that it was Denis Harding who called the Coast Guard.

*

At 6.50pm Denis Harding picks up his mobile phone and rings his wife, Joan. He tells her there's been an accident. She has just heard it on the television. He says he's going to stay out searching for as long as possible.

*

Even though she knows Billy would have eaten something on the boat, Mary O'Connor has the stew on for him. He was due back in Dunmore at 6.00pm and she knows he'll want a hot meal when he gets home. She's sitting in front of a big blazing fire, Rocky at her feet, watching the news when the report about the trawler comes on.

'That's Billy's boat,' Mary says to herself, even though the name of the boat isn't mentioned.

Her first reaction is that Billy is going to be okay because Denis is out there and he'll get them. The next moment, Michael Walsh rings and tells her there's been an accident on Billy's boat. She asks him what she can do.

'Pray,' he says.

When Mary hears this, she knows it must be bad. But she knows her Billy is a brilliant swimmer and is still a fit man. She believes he'll make it. The phone and the doorbell start ringing; people are calling to ask if it's true, to find out if she needs any help. There are questions and tears and more questions and more tears.

*

Michael gets to Dunmore and rings a number of skippers to see who is going out searching. He goes out with Richard Power and they search for the next two to three hours.

'It was equal to at that stage probably as bad a night as I'd ever been at sea in that area,' says Michael. 'You couldn't see your hand. The worst thing is knowing the situation, having been involved in umpteen searches over the years.'

Michael reckons they had no more than four hours to get the men back; he knew Tom was fishing within a window of opportunity and they were getting in ahead of the weather and normally everything would have worked fine.

'I knew what was coming that night and I also knew from previous experiences in that area that if the boys weren't picked up within four hours, it was going to be a job getting them, or getting them alive anyway . . . most of the fishermen went out with that in their mind, it was like the unspoken word, "everybody knew but nobody said," as Christy Moore says.'

*

In Newlyn, Rose Coady is pulling a pint of ale. So far, there are only three customers in 'The Lamp and Whistle', all regulars. Another regular comes in. It's John, who's on crutches because he has two bad hips. He had one of them done, but it's still not right. Rose keeps telling him to go back to the hospital and have it fixed, and he keeps right on ignoring her advice. She gives him his pint.

'God, do you know what, John, I've only cried once this week,' she says.

'Yes Rose, I can see the improvement in you,' says John. 'You're getting a lot better.'

The anniversary of her husband's death is only four days away.

The customers know about Steve and how Rose has suffered in the past twelve months. Just last night the parish priest from Newlyn rang her to ask if she needed anything for the anniversary Mass at the weekend. It's been a very long year for Rose, the longest year of her life. She has never cried as much and is only now beginning to feel alive again.

Her mobile phone rings.

Rose goes over to the phone and looks at it. She picks it up. She puts her other hand to her mouth and gasps. Somebody from Ireland is ringing her. She shakes her head. She just knows something terrible has happened. She puts the phone down without answering it.

'Answer the phone, Rose,' John says.

'No,' she says.

The phone is still ringing.

John and the others tell her to answer it.

Rose picks it up and answers it just before the caller is about to hang up. The man on the other end says he's Bates from Kilmore. She knows him.

'Oh no, please, not again.' Rose is shaking with fear. She knows, she just knows.

'Rose . . . Do I have to tell you?' he says.

'No, not again,' she pleads.

'We've just got word that a boat has gone down off Dunmore, and Patrick is on the boat.'

'I know, I know,' she says, gripping the bar, closing her eyes.

'Rose, I'm so sorry, but I had to tell you, I'm so sorry.'

'No, that's fine, you're grand, don't worry about it,' she manages to say. He gives her the phone number for Michael Walsh, tells her that it's Michael's boat and for her to ring him. Rose doesn't know Michael Walsh. She says she'll ring him and hangs up.

Rose is shaking her head, her legs are buckling, she feels like she's going to faint. The customers know straight away. They get her a chair.

'Oh no, Rose, please don't tell us it's your son?' says John.

Rose nods; she can't talk. She just sits there, her lips quivering, then suddenly she cries an uncontrollable cry, a cry that nobody alive would ever want to hear. A wail that makes grown men weep. It is a cry that comes from some place so deep, there is no name for it. It is the cry of a woman who lost her father-in-law, her husband and now, her only son.

One of the men rings the owner of the pub, who tells them to lock up and bring Rose home.

Over in Wexford, Rose's daughter, Kelly, gets a call on her mobile from a friend.

'Did you hear about the boat going down off the Hook?'

'Jesus, no, I never heard nothing,' says Kelly.

Her friend tells her that the first person they thought of was Patrick.

'But Patrick's not out fishing,' says Kelly.

'Yes he is, he's gone out.'

'Oh my God,' says Kelly. She hadn't known that he was fishing. She tries Patrick's number . . . 'The person you are trying to call may have their mobile switched off . . . ' She tries again and again, but it's just the same message.

She rings her mother in Newlyn.

'I know, I know, Kelly, I know . . . are you okay, Kelly?' asks her Mum.

When Kelly hears this, she knows her brother Pa is gone.

She can't believe it; it's only a year since their father died.

Kelly drives to Hook Head. The wind is fearsome, wild and angry. She can see the beam from the helicopter and the searchlights from the boats. She's never seen the wind as bad as this. She asks a Coast Guard man in an orange jacket if he'd heard who was on the boat.

'I'm not sure, but I heard the name Patrick Coady.'

*

The Coast Guard volunteers in Dunmore are on the headlands, overlooking the estuary. A number of other cars arrive; word is spreading. The wind is so strong that the doors from twelve cars are nearly ripped off their hinges as the doors are being opened. Jim Griffin and his colleagues use a big vice-grips to enable drivers to at least get the doors closed again. The wind and rain is so intense, it's hard for searchers to open their eyes fully.

Down below, the lifeboat is battling the elements, being flung around; it's very difficult to stand; some of the crew fall over or are pushed over by the now 8m (26ft) waves that are careening into the lifeboat. It's a very confused sea. One second they brace themselves for a wave coming in one direction, then suddenly a lump hits them from another side. The weather is so bad that a life-raft from a fishing trawler helping in the search is ripped off by the wind and thrown into the water. They hear Kilmore Quay lifeboat is out, and that friends and colleagues from Fethard-on-Sea and along the coast are risking their lives as well. And it is a big risk, in these conditions.

The lifeboat becomes the on-scene commander, and the crew cannot believe what they are seeing: boat after boat launches out of Dunmore, heading fearlessly out in these atrocious conditions.

Soon there are eight, possibly ten fishing boats on scene. The lifeboat from Kilmore Quay arrives. All the boats follow the orders from the Dunmore lifeboat and with less than half-a-mile between each boat, they form a line and start moving east. All have their full searchlights on and crew members stand on deck, scouring the water for any sign of life.

They can see nothing – no debris patch, no oil.

As the weather worsens, the search is now becoming ineffective. The lifeboat crews physically can't see into the water, such is the amount and power of the wave spray hitting their faces. Suddenly, wind and waves combine in a ferocious punch that sends the Dunmore lifeboat over to a stomch-churning 45° angle. The *Elizabeth and Ronald* is rocked, but gets up off the canvas. It's a 14m (45ft), self-righting 'Trent' class lifeboat, built only ten years ago. It's not going to be bullied off the stage. The sea has knocked off the cover from one of its searchlights at the top of the boat, at least 5m (16ft) up. Ray and his crew are resolute, however: they're not for turning, not yet.

As the wind speed increases, visibility reduces to 0 per cent. The powerful searchlights are now only lighting up the horizontal rain in front of their noses. They can hardly see themselves standing on the deck. The waves are coming in over the lifeboat, forcing every man to cling on to save himself. It's not so much a search-and-rescue mission now as a battle-to-stay-alive mission. They cannot do their job like this.

As on-scene commanders, Ray and his crew have to consider the safety of the other boats out here. A few of the boats that have joined them are smaller than the trawlers, and are taking a terrible battering. It's a terrible admission of defeat, but after some hours searching they have reached the stage when they have to stop. For each and every one of them, it's possibly the hardest decision they've ever made.

*

They somehow get back to the safety of Dunmore harbour at 11.05pm, physically shattered and mentally distraught. Neville Murphy thinks about the lost men, who he'd meet regularly in 'The Butcher's' and 'The Strand'. He can see their faces in his mind's eye and still hopes he'll see them again in the flesh.

In houses all around Dunmore, tears are flowing. Mary O'Connor and her children and their friends and relatives cling to the hope that Billy and the lads may have made it to the life-raft. It's all a terrible, terrible nightmare.

Sarah Maher's heart nearly stopped beating when a friend rang her to say the *Pere Charles* was missing. 'Coady's in it,' she said, a fact her friend hadn't known. Sarah had only just put Treasa to bed a short time earlier, telling her: 'Daddy's still fishing, love, he'll be up to tuck you in the minute he gets home.'

After leaving the lifeboat station, Lulu goes to Gerry Morgan's house. Gerry's a fisherman and his wife, Marie, is a close friend. They turn on the 9 o'clock news and Anne Doyle mentions the name of the boat for the first time. It's only now, in this public announcement, that Lulu feels the full magnitude of what has happened. People have begun arriving at Lulu's mother's house – her brother from Belfast, Tom's brother Johnny from Galway, his other brother Tony driving down from Kildare, Pat Frank and Dan from Kerry, Michael Walsh from the searching. As each one comes in the door, Lulu sheds more tears. She never thought she could cry so much. It's such a sickening feeling, such disbelief. Each face at the door reinforces the shock. But amidst all the tears, they reminisce and try to support each other.

*

Denis Harding and the *Suzanna G* arrive back into Dunmore at around 9.30pm. He tells Pat Frank what Tom said: 'She's broached on me, stand by us.'

'I'd say when he called Denis to stand by him he probably left the wheelhouse, if he had time to leave the wheelhouse before she sank,' says Pat Frank. 'I'd say he sensed there was something not quite right and he would have gone to have a look.' He adds that Tom's natural reaction to the initial 'problem' would have been to slow down the boat.

Pat has spent many years at sea and knows about fishing and weather: 'But none of us have been inside a boat that hit the bottom so quickly. It must have hit the bottom at a fierce impact. We don't know what happens. I mean there could be forces like how fast does the water get in a galley door; is it like a water cannon? Does it blow you and swirl you around, like you'd fill a glass with water out of the tap really quick? Nobody knows, we don't know what happens. Nobody has been through it. The boat was there one minute and she was gone the next. After that we just don't know. We can speculate; Sebastian Junger speculated in *The Perfect Storm*, but he didn't know really either.'

When Marco Power, the man who almost went out, hears the news of the sinking, he's deeply shocked. 'You don't expect experienced guys to go,' he says. 'You'd say things like that don't happen to you and that you'd get out of her but it must have happened so fast, especially as he hadn't the chance to press the distress button and nobody had a chance to get a lifejacket on.'

*

The Coast Guard calls off the search at 11.59pm, to resume at first light. Everybody is bitterly disappointed, but still there is hope that some of the five men must have made it to the life-raft.

Denis and the crew of the *Suzanna G* lock up and go home. They are in a state of shock.

Down on the pier, the Hennessy brothers sit in their car all night, watching the sea.

9

The Fate of the *Honey Dew II*

Sean Bohan is up at 4.00am on Thursday morning. He has heard
about the *Pere Charles* sinking off Dunmore and knows it's a
really bad night. His white milk van shakes and rocks in the wind
as he drives between deliveries. Electricity poles groan, wires move
like skipping ropes and branches break off trees. As he drives, he
keeps one eye on the road and the other on the electricity wires, so
fearful is he of one of them coming down on top of him. He
wonders how Ger is doing out there. Sean worries about him and
he knows his wife, Anne, worries a lot, but he also knows his son
is used to going out in bad weather. He knows he's been out in
Gale Force 11 and even Storm Force 12 in the past; 'he's clever
enough,' thinks Sean, 'he's capable of handling bad weather.'

It's bright now and on his way back home he passes the

harbour, but there's no sign of the *Honey Dew*. He thinks Ger might have sheltered in Ballycotton. In a few minutes he'll meet Mary as she takes the children out to school. He'll ask her if she knows if Ger sheltered anywhere for the night. Mary knows a boat has gone down off Dunmore. She knows that when her Ger heard the news, he would have said: 'Five more souls'. She hasn't heard from Ger, but there is nothing strange in that. She tries ringing him, and Johnny Walsh, and when she can get neither, she expects they are both out of mobile phone range. She expects Ger will ring later in the day. Aneta too tries to ring and text Tomasz, but again, no response. She's sure he'll ring later.

In Dunmore, Lulu hasn't slept at all. There's still no sign of the men or the life-raft and Lulu fears the worst. She goes home before Christine and Jane wake up. She's not planning to tell them anything yet. She turns on the television and sits up on her bed. She's been awake all night and is shattered, emotionally and physically. TV3's 7.00am news comes on. She just can't believe they are talking about her Tom and the boat. It seems so unreal. She hopes it's a bad dream, but it's not. Tom's name is mentioned. Validation. Confirmation. Devastation.

Oh my God, thinks Lulu. And she starts crying, again.

Christine comes into the room and asks her Mammy what's wrong.

It just comes out. Lulu tells her there's been an accident and her Daddy is up in heaven now.

Christine bursts into tears and hugs her Mammy. Both sob.

A few minutes later, Jane gets up and comes in the bedroom door.

In a matter-of-fact tone, Christine says: 'Jane, our Daddy's dead.'

'Is he?' says Jane.

Lulu says: 'Yes, the boat had an accident and isn't coming back and Daddy's in heaven.'

All Jane says is 'Oh.' And then she's silent.

The reports on the television then mention divers going to Dunmore later today, and this confuses the girls as they think the divers are going to bring back Tom and everything is going to be okay.

'If Daddy's up in heaven, why are they looking for him?' says Christine.

Lulu doesn't know what to say; she tries to explain his spirit is gone to heaven. Christine wants to know what his spirit is. Lulu can't think of any word to describe it. She tells her about the kind of person her Daddy was, the way he thought and the way he loved his little girls, 'and that's the part of him that's gone up to heaven and he's watching you now'.

Christine says: 'Can he talk on the mobile phone?'

'No,' says Lulu, 'his phone's all out.'

*

On the *Rachel Jay*, Michael O'Donovan wakes Johnny Walsh at 10.00am. Michael tells him it's been a very bad night.

After a few minutes, Johnny tries to contact Ger on the VHF, but doesn't get any response. This is not unusual as Ger could have been up again during the night and might be back in his bunk now. Johnny thinks nothing of it and says he'll try him again later. They prepare the gear, shoot the nets and then cook some breakfast. Johnny tries Ger again on the VHF, but receives no response. He sends him an email message. After a while, they haul the nets. There's a problem with a lock on one of the trawl doors and it's going to take a few hours to fix.

*

In the bright orange life-raft, Vladimir and Viktor are trying to stay warm. One has a plastic bag over his head to retain heat; the other has two remaining plastic bags over his feet, to minismise heat loss. There's no sign of any boat. They can't see land. All they can see are big waves and grey skies.

Both men are thin, but they are deceptively tough. Their upbringing, their time in the Lithuanian army (with Russian training), Vladimir's years of fishing, both of them having to work hard throughout their lives, all of this contribute to a strong mental attitude and a will to survive. They have been through hell, but they are still alive. They talk about how the boat sank; they can't understand how Tomasz, at least, hasn't made it. They wonder continuously if Ger made it out. They talk about the size of the waves. They discuss whether a container hit them, but agree that if that had happened, the sound may have been somewhat different from what they heard. They try to guess the time, how long they have been bobbing about on this stormy sea. They talk and they wait, and they almost don't dare to hope.

*

Coast Guard teams are out searching from first light. Word comes through that a Spanish fisherman has suffered serious head injuries on a fishing boat 70 miles south-west of Kerry in appalling weather. The RNLI crew from Fenit is dispatched and the man is brought to hospital.

In Waterford, at 10.36am, Rescue 117 relieves the Dublin helicopter, which departs the scene. The Waterford-based crew has more fuel than normal and will stay up searching for a testing three hours and eighteen minutes.

Just as Rescue 117 takes off, there is a major discovery in Wexford: a life-raft and life-ring are spotted at a beach west of Kilmore Quay. The life-raft proves to be empty, however, and there is no sign of anybody near the beach. Teams scour the area both from land and sea, but nothing more is found. The number on the life-raft confirms it's from the *Pere Charles*.

Michael Walsh tells the relatives the heartbreaking news. Shortly afterwards, the life-raft that blew off the searching trawler overnight is also recovered. Men from the diving section of both the Navy and the Garda Síochána arrive in Dunmore to begin preparations for what they expect will be a dive at the wreck. But the wreck hasn't yet been found.

The Sikorsky continues searching. On charts, the crew divides up the Celtic Sea into 'search boxes', each of which is covered extensively. They spend the day going up and down the coastline and further out. There are two pilots up front: one looking down left, the other looking down right. The winch operator is at the door to the right-hand side, looking down and out, while the winchman is seated inside, looking left and back, using the FLIR camera as well as his own eyes. For the four, it's mentally very tiring, this hour upon hour of 'eyeball' searching, but they persevere because they don't want to miss anything. They see the fishing trawlers below all day, operating a creeping line search along the coast. They go back to base at 1.54pm and the engineers perform a very quick turn-around and have the Sikorsky back up in the air by 2.30pm. The crew, two of whom are now Paul Henley and Neville Murphy, will stay airborne until 5.30pm.

Then, in Force 10 winds and high waves, Richard Power on the

Girl Geraldine gets a sonar sounding of what he reckons is the *Pere Charles*, 35m (114ft) below the surface. He drops a shotline and a grapple-hook, which catches maybe a railing on the sunken vessel. The line is marked by a buoy.

*

In Sevastopol, Natalya has been texting Andrey, but receiving no response. She is beginning to worry. It's only a few days since Andrey told her he was going to fish. On the Monday she got a text from him saying there was bad weather. She figures he went back out fishing on the Wednesday. She sends him a lot of text messages, but there's not a single reply. She doesn't know what to do.

*

Johnny Walsh is becoming increasingly worried about Ger. He has tried to get him on the VHF a number of times with no luck, and the messages he's sent via the lap-top have come back as undelivered, which could mean Ger has turned off the power in the boat. But, then, that's something he never does. At 4.30pm Johnny rings Ger's house to see if Mary or the lads have heard from him. Perhaps Ger is back in Kinsale already?

Young James answers the phone.

'Hi James, is your Dad around?'

'No, he's still out fishing,' says James.

'He's still out, is he? I'll give your Mum a ring.'

Johnny doesn't want to alarm James in any way, but this isn't good. He rings Mary on her mobile phone. No, she hasn't heard anything from Ger; she presumes he's still out of range. Johnny tries not to worry her.

*

It's getting dark now and Vladimir and Viktor have been in the life-raft for over thirteen hours. They haven't seen any search boats or rescue helicopter and are very worried they'll have to spend another night on the waves. By this stage they have been thrown about by large waves every few seconds for twenty-four hours; have been soaking wet; have only crackers and water; and now they are fearful they may not be found, especially if they are being dragged further out to sea. They haven't seen one boat all day. They have a flare ready if they sight a boat or helicopter, but so far, nothing.

At 4.55pm Captain Phil Devitt, the Harbour Master in Kinsale, receives a phone call from Eamonn O'Neill, Ger's friend. Mary has told him she's worried. He asks Phil if he can try to find out where the *Honey Dew* is; Phil agrees and rings Naval HQ in Haulbawline. They check their Vessel Monitoring System records and find that the last position they had on him was 11.36pm last night. Phil cannot believe what they are telling him; that's seventeen-and-a-half hours ago.

'Surely you have another position on him?' he says.

'That's the last known one we have,' responds the man on the other end.

'Well, why wasn't somebody alerted to it?'

'I can't comment on that, Phil.'

'Well, try to activate it, send it a signal.'

'Okay.'

The man rings back and tells Phil there has been no response.

'Well in that case,' says Phil, 'we have a major problem because this guy is always in contact with his family and with other fishing boats. Are there any Navy ships in the area?'

'We have the *Emer*, it's on the way up to the *Pere Charles* search, it's off Ballycotton at the moment.'

At this stage, Johnny thinks he sees bits of timber and some netting in the water as he heads towards where Ger was supposed to have been. Phil tells him what the VMS centre has told him. Now Johnny is really worried.

At 5.06pm Johnny gets in touch with the Marine Rescue Coordination Centre in Dublin. He tells them the last contact with Ger was at 1.00am, when the *Honey Dew* was about 6 nautical miles south of Mine Head on the west Waterford coast. The men in MRCC try to contact the *Honey Dew* by VHF and a Pan broadcast is made by Mine Head Coast Guard radio. At no stage was an EPIRB signal received from the *Honey Dew*.

*

Jim Griffin and Ger Hegarty from the Coast Guard are walking down to speak with Richard Power on the pier at Dunmore regarding the exact location of the *Pere Charles*. Ger's phone rings; it's MRCC telling him there's a good possibility that a second boat may be missing; they tell him Johnny Walsh from Kinsale has being trying to contact him all day. Richard Power comes out of the wheelhouse of his boat to talk to them and they ask him if he knows the *Honey Dew*. 'Of course,' he says. They tell him Johnny Walsh has been trying to contact the vessel. Richard says that if Johnny can't get him, Ger is in bother because Johnny is so accurate.

When Joan Bowe hears the news, she just can't believe it. Nobody can. Denis Harding is walking up the pier when he sees Nicko Murphy running towards the RNLI station.

'Where are you off to?' shouts Denis.

'There's been another disaster, the *Honey Dew* is gone.'

Denis knows the boat, he knows Ger to see, but doesn't know him personally. This can't be happening: a second one? It's not possible.

Dunmore is now enveloped in darkness and depression. At 5.27pm the coastal and sea searches are officially suspended for the night and will resume tomorrow. None of the five missing men from the *Pere Charles* has been found, and now there's talk of another boat gone missing.

In Kinsale, Aneta is home with her two children doing homework around 5.30pm when Sean Bohan, Ger's father, comes up the driveway. She knows there must be something wrong. He tells her the boat is missing.

She nearly collapses.

Then she just cries and cries.

Voitek and Alexandria both start to cry, too.

Mother, son and daughter hold each other and weep as their worst fears are realised. Tomasz is missing.

*

At 5.40pm the MRCC launches an official search for the *Honey Dew II*. The LE *Emer* will act as On-Scene Commander; the captain is asked to head for the last-known location of the *Honey Dew* instead of going to Dunmore East. The RNLI crew attached to Ballycotton lifeboat in Cork is also bleeped.

The SAR helicopter is back into Waterford Airport only ten minutes and the crew is looking forward to a hot meal; they've been searching in vain for hours. The engineers are refuelling and doing all the necessary checks on the Sikorsky. Suddenly, the call comes in about the *Honey Dew*. To say there is disbelief would be a gross understatement. The crew of Rescue 117 doesn't even have time for a cup of tea; Neville butters two slices of bread and takes it with him as they run back out to the Sikorsky. Rescue 117 is back out again. It's 5.45pm.

*

The Dunmore East lifeboat crew is making its way back to the harbour after a fruitless day of searching. The crew is absolutely exhausted by the time they reach dry land at 6.00pm. A reporter tells Peter Curran about the *Honey Dew*. He just cannot believe it. It is utterly incredible.

The Coast Guard teams also arrive back, equally exhausted having spent hours on cliff-tops and trudging across fields and beaches, constantly scanning the water and the shore. They are physically and mentally drained. Jim tells them to go home for some food, but to come back afterwards. He tells them he has bad news for them: there could be another search about to be launched.

*

The main evening television news for RTÉ is about to be broadcast live from the steps of the Fishermen's Co-op in Dunmore East. Just before the bulletin goes on air, word comes through that a second boat is missing. The story is double-checked quickly; everybody is shaking their heads in disbelief. Five men being lost is unthinkable, and now, more missing . . .

Rescue 117 has been asked to search from the last-known position of the *Honey Dew* (6 miles south of Mine Head) right down to Kinsale; 'a massive search area,' thinks Neville, 'this is pure needle-in-a-haystack scenario.'

It's dark now and the Sikorsky drops lower as it approaches the

Skipper Tom Hennessy, who died in the tragic sinking of the Pere Charles, on the deck of a trawler off Dunmore a few years before he began skippering the Pere Charles.

Inset: Boat owner Michael Walsh with Johnny Clunny in the wheelhouse of the Pere Charles.

Tom and fiancée Lulu Doyle, with their two children, Christine and Jane.

Above: Ger Bohan, Honey Dew II *owner, who was lost in the tragic sinking, waving from the wheelhouse of his boat and, inset, in the wheelhouse.*

Below: Mary and Ger Bohan in happy times.

Three generations of fishermen lost to the sea.

Left: Paddy Coady and his wife, Mary Ellen.

Middle: Stephen and Rose Coady.

Bottom: Pere Charles crew member Patrick 'Pa' Coady.

Lost Pere Charles *crew member Pat Hennessy, photographed with his niece.*

Fellow crew members, who also died in the tragedy: Billy O'Connor, on a fishing trip in the 1990s, right, and, below, Andrey Dyrin, with wife Natalya and baby Varvara.

Above: Pere Charles

Right: Suzanna G *skipper Denis Harding.*

Below: Honey Dew II

Honey Dew II *crew member Tomasz Jagly, who died in the sinking, on holiday with his wife Aneta and their children Voitek and Alexandria.*

Survivors: Honey Dew II *crew members Viktor Losev and Vladimir Kostvr arrive back at Waterford Airport after being rescued.*

As the search and recovery operation continues, anguished relatives and friends wait by the quayside in desperate hope.

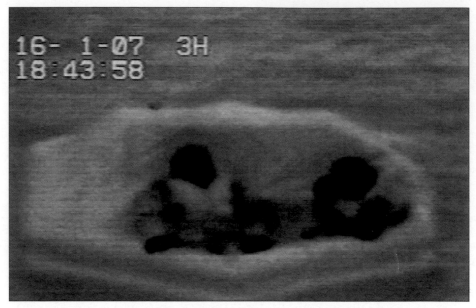

16- 1-07 3H
18:43:58

Infra red image, captured by the Irish Coast Guard helicopter crew, of Renegade *survivors minutes before they were rescued.*

Below: Tom Hennessy, *who lost his son and his brother on the* Pere Charles, *at the Memorial Wall to those lost at sea in Dunmore East.*

last-known position of the *Honey Dew*. The chopper is maybe 2.5 miles from that position. The pilot had transited to it at 305m (1,000ft), but now drops down to 60m (200ft). The crew is not expecting to see anything yet . . . if they are going to see anything at all.

Down below, the wind has abated a little; Vladimir thinks he hears something; it's very faint, but it sounds like a helicopter. Is his mind playing tricks on him? He asks Viktor if he can hear it. He tears open the zip . . . YES, up there, look, in the distance, the flashing lights . . . it must be a helicopter. *Quick!* It looks like they are heading past; they're going to miss us; quickly, the flare . . .

Vladimir grabs the flare and lights it. It shoots up into the night sky, burning bright red. It has a small parachute attached and it should stay up there for maybe 30 seconds before burning out and falling down into the water.

Vladimir and Viktor stare at the flare, then at the helicopter, then back at the flare, and back again at the helicopter; it's not turning round, it's flying on. The men shout and wave frantically, but they know their potential rescuers are miles away. If they don't see the flare, they might have lost their one and only chance of rescue. A few more anxious seconds pass, the flare is beginning to lose power, they're not going to see it . . .

The survivors are right: Rescue 117 is not going in the direction of the life-raft. It's heading towards the last-known position of the *Honey Dew*; the life-raft has been blown nearly 3 miles further out to sea. The crew is looking ahead for the *Honey Dew*, not behind for a momentary streak of light from a flare.

Paul Truss is winchman for this flight. He's looking at his monitor, which is showing him infrared pictures of the sea below. They are not actually searching at this stage, just transiting to the location to begin their search. Neville Murphy is standing at the cockpit door, talking via the intercom in his helmet to the two pilots. He has no reason to turn around and look out of one of the windows on the left side of the Sikorsky; he has no reason to look behind; he can't see anything out there; it's pitch black; you can't even see the waves below it's now so dark. But for some reason, a reason to this day he thinks must have been fate, Neville Murphy does look out and back to his left. And there, in the distance, he sees a red flare dropping in an arc.

'Lads, flare, eight o'clock,' he shouts into his helmet intercom.

Immediately, pilot Captain Mark McDermott banks the machine hard left and for a second, he and the co-pilot can see the flare dead ahead. But then suddenly it disappears, and everything goes black again. The flare has burnt out and hit the water.

The crew makes a quick calculation – yes, it's definitely at least 5 miles away. The head straight there, not knowing who released the flare or from where exactly it was released, just knowing what they've seen – and that someone has to have put up the flare from the water.

Neville can't believe he saw it. He knows a flare has a life of around 30 seconds and that there was less than 10 seconds left from the time he saw it and the time it disappeared. He had seen it at the top of its arc; it was already going back down as the helicopter was turning, and then it was gone.

'Lucky' is a word rescue men don't use lightly, but it seems luck is shining on Vladimir and Viktor. They see the helicopter turn towards them; they can't believe it; they must have seen the flare at the last second. The two men stand up and shout and scream even louder. They have to be careful not to get washed overboard because there is still quite a 'lump' in the sea, but they are utterly desperate to make themselves seen, to make their voices heard.

The helicopter is nearing where the crew thinks the flare must have come from.

Paul Truss suddenly shouts, 'Life-raft, dead ahead, two people on board.' Through the infra-red camera he has picked up the heat source from the two men in the raft, far below them.

The helicopter approaches. The waves are still big, maybe 3–5m (10–16ft), and there is still 30 knots of wind, but it's not as bad as it was sixteen, or even twelve hours ago. They fly straight over the life-raft, flashing lights as they do to let the men know they've seen them. It's procedure to do a circuit and come back down to a certain height.

The four crew men have a quick briefing as to how they are going to handle the situation. The only way they are going to rescue the men is by using what is known as a 'high-line'. This is where they throw a rope down to the men in the life-raft, they grab it and pull it towards them. The winchman then goes down the rope as the men in the raft pull him towards them. It means the helicopter will have to work directly over the men. By hovering directly overhead, a slight filter will be created that should minimise the effects of the downwash from the helicopter, which otherwise will push the life-raft away from the helicopter. They know it's not going to be an easy task: taking anybody out of a moving life-raft on a rough sea is tricky enough, but taking somebody out of a life-raft on a rough sea at night is very difficult. The main problem is that the pilots have no reference points; they are hovering over a black expanse. For this sort of manoeuvre, it's all about staying calm, drawing on experience and holding her steady and level until the job is done.

They move in over the men and throw down the rope. Vladimir catches it. Paul lowers himself down the line, and Vladimir and Viktor pull him into the life-raft. Paul gives them the thumbs-up sign; they respond in kind. Paul puts the harness on them and indicates that both of them will be going up together. It takes four to five minutes to get the both of them up, during which time Paul stays on the raft to ensure they get up safely. As they are going up, neither Vladimir nor Viktor talks; they are so nervous and cold. But when Neville helps them into the helicopter, broad smiles light up their dishevelled faces. 'Yes, we are alive now,' they think.

Paul gets winched back up to safety.

It's 6.30pm.

There are thumbs-up all round. The two men are wrapped in blankets. The pilots radio the LE *Emer*, which they know is approximately 6 miles away. They give the position of the life-raft. The LE *Emer* will later pick up the small orange rubber inflatable that has saved these men's lives.

In the back of the Sikorsky, communications between the two Lithuanians and Neville and Paul are proving difficult. It's a very noisy environment inside the helicopter and the men's pidgin English is proving a major hindrance. Vladimir and Viktor try to smile as much as possible and keep saying 'thank you' over and over. Neville asks them questions and manages to ascertain that they spent many hours in the life-raft. He asks them how many hours. They say maybe seventeen, based on their estimated timing between when the boat sank and when dusk fell. Neville and Paul can't believe they are so healthy after what they have been through. They check them physically, but there are no visible medical concerns; they're a bit cold, but their body temperature is not alarming; their pulse and respiratory rates are normal; there is no need to use the heart monitor. Neville tells the Captain that the survivors are okay. This information is radioed back to MRCC in Dublin.

'Two survivors, confirmed; two crew members still missing.'

*

The news spreads rapidly that two men have been rescued alive. Johnny Walsh gets the report and tells Mary Bohan. Everyone is trying to find out who the survivors are. Mary's emotions go from a massive high when she hears there are survivors, to a crashing low when she's told that neither of them is Ger. But it does at least allow her to hope; if two have been found, maybe Ger and Tomasz are safe also.

Within five minutes it's reported live on the television news bulletins: both RTÉ and TV3 announce that two men have been found alive and that the search for the other two crew members is continuing.

*

As Vladimir and Viktor are not in need of immediate hospital care, and as they said they wanted to stay searching for Ger and Tomasz, Rescue 117 recommences its search. The crew is delighted to have two survivors and feel they now have a chance of finding the other two men somewhere. They also know that another helicopter (Rescue 116, from Dublin) is en route, as is the LE *Emer* and the Ballycotton and Dunmore lifeboats.

Neville and Paul keep trying to get more information from Vladimir and Viktor that might help the search. Viktor has some English, but not much. He mentions something about a life-ring, but Neville and Paul are finding it hard to understand the meaning of what he's trying to say. They continue searching at the optimal search height, 60m (200ft); the FLIR is the main 'eye' for the helicopter at night, while all the men on board scan the waters below for anything at all. A short while later they get a radio communication telling them that the members of Ballycotton lifeboat have picked up a second life-raft. It's empty.

Rescue 117 continues searching until around 8.30pm, but now that the second raft has been found empty, there is a growing realisation that the skipper and his crewmate have probably drowned. They touch down at Waterford Airport at 8.48pm and Vladimir and Viktor walk gingerly with Neville and Paul to the crew building. Photographers and reporters are waiting. Inside, they watch as the 9.00pm news relates what has happened.

These are two very lucky men.

*

Johnny Walsh is still out on the *Rachel Jay*, looking for Ger and Tomasz. He thinks about last night, about the fact that there were probably no more than six boats out fishing on the south and south-east coast (a fact that is later confirmed). He feels very angry when he thinks of the VMS operated by the Navy: why didn't they know the *Honey Dew* was gone? They should have known. It's not like there were forty or fifty boats out and they missed it amongst many others. And given that the weather was so bad last night and the *Pere Charles* had sunk, surely they should have been thinking, 'How are the other boats doing?'

Johnny thinks about the fact that the Navy boys were able to ring Ger on the Tuesday morning after he had powered down the boat for an hour for some welding, but they couldn't ring Mary all day today if they knew the VMS was not responding from the

Honey Dew II. Their last record of Ger was just before midnight, there had been no trace of the boat all day and yet they still hadn't called anyone. Johnny knows it's not their fault that Ger hasn't been found, but he can't help thinking that the search-and-rescue mission could have been launched a lot quicker if the VMS had been used differently.

As it's constituted at present in Ireland, the VMS is not a system to monitor safety at sea. It is a system to monitor and prevent over-fishing. What happened is that on Thursday morning, those boats from which a VMS signal weren't transmitted were checked by a member of the Navy team at Haulbawline (there can be up to fifteen missed reports each day). He phoned Ger Bohan's mobile, but obviously couldn't get him and tried ringing him three or four times throughout the day. Mary Bohan says that in the past they rang her at home to ask about the VMS being turned off, but the Navy says the only contact number for Ger on that Thursday morning was his mobile.

*

The cold and bitter wind is forcing people to huddle closer on the quayside in Kinsale. At one stage, close on twenty people are gathered at the small quay wall. Some say prayers; others talk about the missing men, about their chances of being found alive. For Mary Bohan and Aneta Jagly it's their worst imaginable nightmare. Neither of them sleeps a wink that night and early the following morning both are down on the quay.

Mary gazes out across the stormy waters. She can't contain her grief any longer. She sobs, 'Bring him home, bring him home, I want him back home.'

Newspapers will report that families divided by culture and

language are now united in grief. And that while the past few days rank as the blackest in living memory for the Irish fishing industry, these two women, Mary and Aneta, offer inspiration through their remarkable courage and solidarity.

In the local church, Canon O'Mahony says Mass and speaks of his own experience of death at sea: 'There were three young people drowned in Dunmanway Bay. I remember an old man comforting the wives of those men. He did it quietly, he wasn't a scholarly man but he had a great faith. One of the women was complaining why God would do it. He told her she didn't deserve what she had to go through but he compared her to Mary at the cross.'

Other family members have told Canon O'Mahony that they hope God is deaf, because they don't want him to hear all the things they have said since the tragedy.

Some fishermen talk about how the *Honey Dew* was on the water for twenty years and that it was a great boat. After Mass, some of the men kiss their girlfriends and wives and then head out in their boats to search for Ger and Tomasz.

*

In Sevastopol, Natalya Dyrin receives a phone call and is told there has been a fishing tragedy in Ireland. She is shocked, but she already knew something was wrong because Andrey hasn't been in touch.

The phone rings again. This time it's somebody from the Ukraine foreign office; he tells her the news.

Natalya is standing beside Andrey's mother, who sees Natalya's expression and knows something is terribly wrong. Suddenly, Natalya's entire body feels numb, her head feels empty and she is full of tears. She and Andrey's mother become extremely weak and collapse; an ambulance is called. Andrey's mother is in such a state of shock she seems paralysed and cannot speak.

The Council of Ukraine rings again later, when Natalya has returned from the hospital, and ask if she wants to travel to Ireland. She says she does. She pays for her flight herself, but is promised a refund from the government. A special visa is approved in only two hours (usually it takes six months). She can't take her daughter with her because she doesn't have a passport, so she will stay with her grandparents. The only thing on Natalya's mind now is to find Andrey. When she arrives in Waterford she goes to Dunmore and, that night, she insists upon sleeping in Andrey's bed in the house in which he has been renting.

*

From Wednesday evening and all through Thursday, people call to the Coast Guard station and the RNLI building on the quay and leave in plates of sandwiches, cakes they've baked, milk, biscuits and all sorts of food. There are unsung heroes all around, none more so than the Ladies Guild of the RNLI, who make soup, tea and sandwiches for all-comers, operating shifts to make sure everyone is catered for.

Over the next few days, Jim Griffin is amazed and inspired by the camaraderie he witnesses across the towns of the area. The help and support offered from people all across the country is overwhelming. Jim knows there's never been anything like it, and hopes there will never have to be anything like it again. Dozens of people ring the Coast Guard station offering free B&B to anyone who has travelled to take part in the searches. Others take it upon themselves to go walking on beaches from Ardmore, in west Waterford, to Curracloe on the east Wexford coast; they ring the station and tell them they are going to walk so far and if they see anything, they'll report back. Rescue services from Inland Waterway Units from as far away as Lough Derg, dog and mountain rescue teams, climbing teams from the Comeraghs, all offer their services. One 'ordinary' person who offers help is an employee in the Guinness brewery at St James's Gate in Dublin. He has a holiday home in Waterford. When he gets a few days off work, he drives down, walks into the Coast Guard station and says he wants to help search. After a day searching, he leaves his phone number with Jim, hands him the set of keys to his summer house, gives him the code to his alarm and says if anyone needs the house, let them stay there.

'Where do you get better than that?' says Jim.

*

For those involved in the search for the *Honey Dew*, the mission has now become a recovery as opposed to a rescue operation. The second, empty life-raft from the *Honey Dew II* is located at 10.00am on Friday morning, 12 January off Ballycotton in east Cork. In these conditions a man might realistically last six hours in a survival suit, but now, especially after the second raft has been found empty, all hope of finding anybody alive is lost. Organisationally, however, the operation does not change and the number of searches is not stepped down. In fact, it's increased. But the families are told what they know in their hearts already: it's not expected to find any more survivors.

In Dunmore, six RNLI volunteers stride out onto the steel gangway in their distinctive yellow overalls and put out to sea.

138

'That's sheer bloody courage,' says a local Garda.

Throughout the day, blue wooden planks, Wellington boots, some wheelhouse gear, including computer screens, and other items from the *Honey Dew II* are found along the coastline. Everything that is found is brought to the Coast Guard station in Dunmore and Jim Griffin has the awful task of asking fishermen who knew the boat to come in and identify the items.

Involved in the sea searches on Friday are over twenty trawlers and fishing boats, the LE *Emer*, plus lifeboats from Rosslare, Kilmore Quay, Dunmore East and Ballycotton. From the shore, searches will be carried out by Coast Guard teams from Carnsore, Kilmore Quay, Fethard, Dunmore East, Tramore, Bunmahon, Helvick Head and Ardmore. Relatives and members of the public also take part, as do members of the Gardaí. Fishing vessels that help in the search for Ger and Tomasz and the *Honey Dew* include the *Carmona*, the *Cu na Mara*, the *Ocean Pioneer*, the *Rachel Jay*, the *Buddy M*, the *Sean Mair II*, the *Silver Harvest*, the *Western Venture* and the *Johnny K*.

In spite of all this, there is still no location for the *Honey Dew II*; Viktor and Vladimir aren't sure of their last-known position before the destruction of the vessel.

An idea of how intense a search operation this has become is clear from looking at the log-book at the Bunmahon Coast Guard, meticulously updated by Colin Dwan and Seamus Power. They organise three search teams (Alpha, Bravo and Charlie), with two qualified members in each. They all meet at 7.45am at their small station in Bunmahon and begin searching at 8.35am. There is a total of fifty-five 'records of action' in the Bunmahon log-book alone; every other Coast Guard unit would have just as much information. They are joined by volunteers from Kinsale at

9.40am, including Sean Bohan and others members of Ger's family. By 10.05am Dunmore Coast Guard has found two items of clothing at Coolum Cove, near Ballymacaw. At 2.48pm a blue jumper is washed onto the beach at Bunmahon. By 4.36pm all volunteers and teams have returned safely to base. At 4.45pm, the search is called off for the night.

10

Locating the *Pere Charles*

The searches for the *Honey Dew* and the crew of the *Pere Charles* are carried on simultaneously. In Dunmore, where the Coast Guard is still focused on finding the five crew members of the *Pere Charles*, Jim Griffin, Joan Bowe and Ger Hegarty are back in the station at 7.00am on the Thursday morning. They want to get the teams going again as early as possible. It's a massive logistical effort to ensure every crack and crevice along the coast is searched, areas where they know debris or rubbish are washed into after storms. On their charts and maps they identify the areas that must be searched according to priority. They phone team leaders in neighbouring stations, such as Bunmahon, Tramore, Fethard-on-Sea, Kilmore Quay and Carnsore. The forecast is bad, with winds up to Force 10 forecast; they won't be able to get any of their inflatable ribs out in those sea conditions.

They head across the road to the Ocean Hotel for a meeting with bleary-eyed relatives, volunteers, trawler skippers and RNLI members. Everybody is briefed. Coast Guard units equipped with binoculars head for the dangerous cliffs and headlands, to look for anything that might give them a clue as to the five men's whereabouts. As the prevailing winds are south-westerly, anybody who managed to get out of the *Pere Charles* would have been pushed eastwards along the south Wexford coast.

Denis Harding says that he's going back out to search. He tells Pat Frank Hennessy and his brothers; they don't need to be told twice. Within a few minutes, they are on the *Suzanna G*, headed for the final resting place of the *Pere Charles*. They all crane their necks and scan the water. The weather is so bad they have to hunker down. They don't see anything. Other boats come out to help, including the *Renegade* owned by Kevin Downes from Duncannon. Dunmore lifeboat is out at 8.24am. Its crew plans to stay out all day until they find something, or someone. Kilmore Quay lifeboat is also out with a full crew, as is the RNLI lifeboat from Rosslare. Overhead, the Coast Guard helicopter from Dublin has flown down to help search for the missing men.

*

Down on the quayside in Dunmore, relatives are using the RNLI as a meeting centre. Reporters and photographers are milling around, trying to get interviews and photographs. Television camera crews are doing likewise. Michael Walsh tells reporters that he's totally devastated by the loss of the *Pere Charles*. When asked what he thinks might have caused the tragedy, he replies, 'A freak wave got it, a series of unfortunate events; whatever happened, happened in a split-second; I don't think the [fish] catch would have slipped and unbalanced the boat. We'd only fitted out the boat with new timbers; I think he was in control and something else hit the boat.'

Julia and Tom Hennessy (Tomaisín's parents) arrive from Kerry. They hug Mary O'Connor when they are introduced. They have never met before. They never wanted to meet like this. Everybody cries.

It's exceptionally hard for the families with so many reporters, television cameras and photographers always present. A television camera can film from a somewhat discreet distance, but many of the photographers walk right up to relatives and *snap/snap/snap* in their faces with a lens a foot long. So intrusive is the media presence that a sign is erected on the RNLI station that no members of the media are permitted to enter. While the Coast Guard officers realise that people all over the country genuinely want to know what is going on, it doesn't detract from the fact that some relatives feel harassed by the attention.

A few days' later, one of the many cards and messages of support which arrive at the RNLI office comes with a parcel of Twix bars and Cadbury Creme Eggs. The card reads: 'To the searchers, thank you for looking for my daddy and the other fishermen . . . hope you like the food'. It's from James Bohan, aged ten, from Kinsale.

*

Once Richard Power had located the wreck of the *Pere Charles* by throwing down the grapple-hook and placing a marker, the next task is to get an official reading from sonar sounding and then get divers down to see if any of the men are still trapped inside. However, members of the Garda Water Unit, Coast Guard officers and Navy divers reckon it will be a few days before it will be possible to search the boat. One of the divers says that while they can dive in swells of up to 2m (6.5ft), a 5m (16ft) swell can throw up 7m (22ft) waves, which is unsafe diving conditions; but he says optimistically and resolutely, 'We'll bring them home, it might take days or longer, but we'll bring the lads home.'

Finally, in mid-afternoon on the Friday, confirmation comes through that the *Pere Charles* has been officially identified as lying in 35m (114ft) of water, not far from where the EPIRB was found.

At 4.30pm Irish naval vessel the LE *Eithne* arrives at the scene after a gruelling twenty-eight-hour journey from northwest Donegal; it will take over as the on-scene commander. It comes in close to Dunmore and a naval dinghy takes Lt Tony O'Regan of the Naval Service Diving team from Dunmore to the *Eithne*. They head out to assess the wreck site. Lt O'Regan confirms there will be no diving tomorrow, and probably not for a few days, because of the continuing large swell.

*

The President of Ireland, Mary McAleese, issues a statement expressing her sadness at the terrible tragedies:

> 'Our thoughts are with those families still awaiting news of those who are still missing. It is indeed good news that at least two men have survived. The work of our rescue services, who are clearly making every effort in appalling weather conditions, was critical in ensuring the survival of these men.'

*

Saturday, 13 January, and the *Honey Dew II* still hasn't been found, but more and more wreckage from the trawler is washing up along the Waterford and Wexford coasts. Fishermen fear the boat is now breaking up. The wreckage ranges from splintered shards of planking to fish boxes and netting gear and is being reported found on coastal areas all around Mine Head as conditions finally begin to ease after four days of gale force winds and 5m (16ft) high swells. Some of the wreckage is recovered nearly 50 miles away from the last-known location of the *Honey Dew*.

Coast Guard officers make contact with their English and Welsh counterparts and formally request that all fishermen be on the lookout for bodies over the coming weeks. At this stage, many believe that most, if not all, of the five men from the *Pere Charles* are still in the sunken vessel. But with debris from the *Honey Dew* travelling so far, Coast Guard officials fear that strong currents may have swept the bodies of Ger and Tomasz out into St George's Channel and the Irish Sea. It isn't unknown for bodies to wash up ten to twelve days after an incident, even sometimes a month after going missing.

*

Viktor and Vladimir insist on travelling to Kinsale for the special prayer service organised for Ger and Tomasz. They tell reporters (through an interpreter) that the boat was destroyed by a wave that must have been at least 14m (45ft) high; that it must have caused immense and immediate damage to the side of the wooden boat; that Ger Bohan had made a desperate attempt to issue a SOS alert.

As they walk into the church for their prayer service, people stop and stare, wondering if these are the survivors. A few recognise them; suddenly, people start clapping. Within two seconds the entire congregation is on its feet, applauding the men as they walk up towards the front. The men don't know how to feel. They embrace Mary Bohan and Aneta Jagly. Many people are crying.

*

On Sunday, the bad weather continues, with winds gusting from Force 7 to Force 9. Again, hundreds of people take part in searches, but there is nothing to report, neither at sea nor from the shore. People drive or get lifts from all over the country to help search. The divers have to abort another attempt to dive at the wreck of the *Pere Charles*. The Coast Guard asks the Irish Lights Vessel, the *Granuaile*, to make its way to Dunmore to act as a diving platform for the Navy divers, if and when they get a chance to dive.

On Saturday evening the line and buoy that Richard Power put down to mark the location of the *Pere Charles* broke, so on Sunday morning the Kilmore Coast Guard rings Jim Griffin to tell him they have recovered it. The destruction of the marker shows the strength of the wind and tides, and that everything is travelling in the same direction.

Transport Minister Martin Cullen and Junior Transport Minister Pat the Cope Gallagher arrive to meet with the families of the seven missing fishermen and to personally pledge the Government's full support to recovering their bodies and investigating the cause of the double tragedy. Minister Gallagher worked as a fish exporter for twelve years in Donegal, so he knows the sea and the havoc it can wreak on people's lives. Together, the two tragedies involve four countries – Ireland, Ukraine, Lithuania and Poland – and between them the seven missing men leave fifteen children fatherless. It's the kind of tragedy that will have repercussions for years to come.

*

On Monday 15 January, searches resume at first light and even though hundreds again take part, there is nothing to report. The wind eases off slightly to a Force 6, but it's still too choppy for diving. Fishing trawlers, including the *Renegade*, continue to look for the missing crewmen off the Waterford and Wexford coasts.

As the searching continues, the Coast Guard makes an important decision in the search to locate the *Honey Dew*: it passes over to local trawlers the responsibility of recommending which areas should be searched. Johnny Walsh has been out searching for days. He's tired, but happy that they can now use their local knowledge to try to find Ger's boat.

*

On Tuesday, winds moderate to Force 3 or 4, but are due to increase to Force 6 and maybe Force 7 in the evening.

Nonetheless, the divers from the Irish Navy are going to try to dive the *Pere Charles*. The men get their gear ready on the *Granuaile*, under the watchful eye of Lt Darragh Kirwan, the officer in charge of the Naval Diving Unit. His diving unit consists of twenty-three members (all men, although it is open to women), of which about fifteen are here in Dunmore.

The unit is well-equipped, although each dive is different, the depths involved determining what equipment is necessary. For this dive, the Navy has a huge amount of equipment because they are going to use Surface Applied Diving Equipment, i.e. helmets, heavy vests and umbilicals attached to the divers. The cut-off point at which divers change from normal scuba-diving gear to this heavier gear is 35m (114ft) and as the *Pere Charles* is lying in 34–36m (111–118ft) of water, they are using the heavier stuff, which is more labour-intensive, involves more people and requires a diving platform and a larger amount of back-up.

Lt Kirwan is very conscious of the safety of his men, and is being extra careful because of the extraordinary weather conditions over the past week:

> 'You run the risk of a ground swell. This is where the water is moving from the surface down to the seabed; so if there is 5m swell, the entire water column is moving up and down, as well as water surging back and forth. We've seen a lot of cases where it looks quite decent on the surface, but you don't know what the conditions are like underwater. I know of divers going down 7m, then suddenly, because of the movement inside the water column, being pushed down to 15m and then pulled back up again to 7m. What this can mean is punctured lungs. Then on the seabed you have ground swell also. It's like an invisible punch. I know of a diver who came out of a wreck and was suddenly knocked back metres along the seabed. If you push somebody on land, they might fall back one or two metres, but the water "encapsulates" you and you are thrown back a lot more.'

He is also acutely aware that here, along the south coast, the force of water that was out in the Atlantic is now channelling in on the shallower ground, waves are getting bigger on the surface and maybe the same is happening underwater. There are other potential problems, too, like getting caught in nets and strong tides, particularly in this area.

'You would not be able to swim against a strong tide,' he says. 'A diver would be able to work against a 1 knot to 1.5 knot tide over a long period (depending on his fitness levels and other things), but if you are looking at tides of 3 or 4 knots, it just isn't possible.'

Two naval divers get ready to descend. They are wearing thermal undersuits and a Neopreme 'dry suit' to keep them warm, then a piece that covers their neck (called a neck damp) and a heavy canvas waistcoat that holds the weights and has securing points for whatever the diver needs to take down with him. They wear Neopreme gloves and, for this dive, fins on their feet as opposed to heavy rubber boots. Air is supplied via an air hose, and the diver's head is encased in a heavy helmet; it is so heavy, you can't hold your head up straight without using hands to support it. Out of the water, it looks and is very cumbersome; in the water, it works. The divers can communicate with team leaders on the diving platform via the two-way system on the umbilical. There is also a small camera attached to the helmet, which sends colour pictures to the team leaders above, who can monitor exactly where the diver is going. Each diver also has a cylinder on his back, a back-up system (called the bail-out) should the umbilical sever or leak. All precautions have been observed; they are ready to dive down to the *Pere Charles* and, hopefully, find the bodies of the five crewmen.

The men will work in pairs, and only two divers will descend at any given time because four doing this 'freestyle' diving at the same time could lead to lines getting dangerously entangled, especially as visibility might be only 0.3m (1ft). They work between the tides to minimise the effects of fast water underneath them (it can flow so fast, divers sometimes have to hold onto their descending/ascending rope and are like flags billowing in a strong wind).

The first two men go down, holding onto the rope used to mark the spot by the *Girl Geraldine*. It takes them no more than two minutes to descend the 35m (114ft). Diving conditions are difficult. They only have 0.1–0.3m(0.5–1ft) visibility, but suddenly, the *Pere Charles* is in front of them. It's an eerie sight, even for these experienced divers. The light on their helmets does not provide any peripheral vision. It gives a straight line of light; everything else is black. They can see only what is directly in front of them, and if they turn their heads slightly left or right, they get a completely new perspective. It's very disorientating.

When they reach the vessel, they find that the grapple-hook is latched onto a tyre that was being used as a fender on the port side of the *Pere Charles*. They see that the vessel is lying on its starboard side, over on its side maybe 130°, with the wheelhouse digging into the seabed. Much of it has already been crushed inwards.

The first task is to secure a stronger line, known as a shot line, which they secure to the port side, just ahead of the wheelhouse. Once this is done, the men begin moving inch by inch, looking around the outside of the vessel, trying to get their bearings. At any stage, they may come across a body.

The boat is rocking slightly on the seabed, shifting in the ground swell, and the front end of the wheelhouse is badly damaged. The divers have a look, but can't get in because the damage prevents access to the bridge. They shine in as much light as possible, but can't see any of the men. The deck of the boat has now become a wall. Under regulations, they have only thirty to thirty-five minutes for each dive because if they stay any longer, they will have to take longer coming back up, with stops along the way, in order to recompress. So they return to the surface and let the next team go down.

Two more dives are done over the next few hours. They locate the aft hatch of the wheelhouse, but cannot get in because of debris and ropes. They reach a hatch at the stern; it's at such an angle that the diver is standing beside it, like looking out a window. This is the hatch to the hold where all the herrings should be. It is open, the cover has been blown off for some reason, possibly by the pressure of the water as it sank. One of the divers says he's going to put his head in. He does and is met by total inky blackness; the lamp's light doesn't even penetrate 2 inches. The diver gets a very strong smell of fish (the gases sometimes permeate through the neck damp). He pulls his head back out. Lt Kirwan reckons this could be dangerous.

The team leaders speak with marine biologists to ensure gases like hydrogen sulphide, ammonia and methane aren't a possibility because divers could become unconscious on contact with these and die very quickly. They will pump more air to the divers when they go back to this hatch so that the air will push out whatever gases might be seeping in through the rubber neck seals.

Just as it seems progress is being made, the weather yet again rears up and the dive has to be called off. The *Granuaile* heads for Dunmore shortly after 4.30pm. Worse still, it looks like there won't be another chance of diving for a week as the long-range forecast is predicting south-west gales until Saturday, followed by north-westerly gales.

The divers report to the Coast Guard officials, and to Michael

Walsh and the relatives, that none of the men has been recovered in any of these initial three dives, nor was there any sighting of the bodies. The relatives are devastated. The whole community is devastated. This nightmare really does seem to be unending.

11

A Third Boat Sinks

The scramble phone rings in Waterford Airport SAR. It's just after 5.00pm on Tuesday 16 January and the caller is from Marine Rescue in Dublin.

'We have a vessel in difficulty, the *Renegade*, they are abandoning ship and launching into a life-raft, it's past Tuskar Rock, around 10 miles past Tuskar Rock.'

The longitude and latitude points are given and the SAR officer on duty, Captain Dara Fitzpatrick, hits the scramble bell and the claxon goes off all through the building, hangar and outside. Dara and her colleagues – Mark McDermott, Neill McCadden, Keith Devanney, Barry Cahill and Declan McHenry – are needed yet again; it's been a long week.

The engineers put 700lbs of extra fuel into the Sikorsky, enough for a further forty minutes' flying. They do this because the weather is deteriorating and it's quite rare to find survivors straight away on scene; they tend to have to search for them, which could last an hour or more. The crew race to get into their orange suits. As they're doing this, they're saying to one another, 'This is unreal, it can't be true, it can't be happening again . . . three boats in just one week, it's very, very strange.' They are airborne within seven minutes of taking the call.

Denis Harding and his crew on the *Suzanna G* are on their way into Dunmore after a long day searching. They are around 2 miles from the Hook when word comes over on Channel 16 that the *Renegade* is sinking 27 miles away; Denis turns the boat around and start steaming for the location. Denis is grim at the wheel – three boats in six days, in all his life he's never seen anything like it.

In Dunmore, word is seeping out that yet another boat is sinking. Jim Griffin and the Coast Guard teams are astounded. They are debriefing in the station when a call comes in from MRCC: 'Stand by again.'

This is a bizarre turn of events.

They hear the position is off Tuskar, so the initial indication is that it won't involve this team, 'but you just never know,' says Jim.

It's max. speed for Rescue 117 from the airport to Tuskar Rock. Winchman Keith Devanney is listening to Channel 16 on the radio and can hear the Coast Guard talking to the men on the boat, but can't hear the response. He and his colleagues know there are two men in the life-raft and that they have abandoned ship. They know this is serious. They also know there's a big cargo vessel, the *Euphoria*, not far away that may be able to help if the men can't be found. Dara steers the helicopter past Carnsore and down to 152m (500ft). It's very dark. They can see the lights of the cargo vessel, but they can't see the *Renegade*. Keith is on the Fleur, looking for the vessel with the infrared camera, scanning 20° either side of the aircraft. Mark McDermott tells them they are at the 5-mile point, and a few seconds later the Fleur picks up the heat from two men in a dome shape, which must be the life-raft. Now they can all see the *Renegade*, which is listing slightly to the port side.

Dara engages the over-fly system: they fly straight over the top of the life-raft, press the over-fly button and the aircraft works out what speed and direction the wind is blowing and does a racetrack pattern all the way back around and puts itself in a hover position into the wind, over the raft. Often they don't use the full over-fly system, but this time they decide to let the system do it as they can see the two men, who are hopefully alive and well. The sinking boat is in the foreground. They radio the cargo vessel nearby to continue on its present course 'so as to clear the operating area'. They discuss how they are going to perform the rescue. Keith makes his way to the door, checks his equipment, connects himself onto the high line, gives the thumbs-up and is away out the door. The chopper is hovering at 12m (40ft). Keith gives the special 'height good' wave and Dara goes back up to 21m (70ft).

Keith is the eyes of the operation because at this stage, Dara can't see the life-raft as it's directly underneath; all she can see are the two landing lights on the helicopter and then pitch black beyond. She looks at the Doppler hover metre on her instrument panel: when the cross is in the middle, the Sikorsky is in hover position.

'Forward and right 5.'

Everything has to be very stable; there are 17 or 18 knots of wind. At least it's not raining.

'Steady.'

Trying to maintain a steady hover with no visual references is tricky.

'Forward 2.'

The downwash is catching the life-raft and pushing it forward a little.

Neil McAdam directs Dara towards the raft. The waves are now reaching heights of between 3m and 4m (10ft and 14ft). Keith doesn't want to go too low too quickly because a wave can come up and hit him or land on him, which can be quite painful depending on the size of the wave; 'it can be like hitting a wall'. They get close to the raft and Keith hits the water before hoisting himself into the raft. He gives the thumbs-up to Neil McAdam, unhooks himself and lets the winch go back up to the helicopter. He turns to the two men: 'Hello, how are you? I'm Keith.'

The first man, Ken Doyle, says he's fine and is happy to see him. Kevin Downes, the *Renegade*'s skipper, is slightly more subdued. Keith does an initial medical check on both and briefs them on what a 'high line' rescue involves. Neil McAdam drops down the weighted bags with a high line rope attached to the hook; Keith then feeds in the rope at his feet as the aircraft moves back. Neil winches out again; Keith pulls in the excess rope until he gets the hook in his hand. Attached to the hook is a strop, which goes around Ken, who puts his hands on the buckle and holds on. Keith then gives him the handle from the high line to help him steady himself once he takes off on his 21m (70ft) journey to safety because he's taking off at a slight angle. Keith will add tension to the rope as Ken is hoisted up in order to cancel out the swing.

Once Ken is safely in the helicopter, the cable comes down

again and Kevin is stropped on. Keith dumps the high line because they don't need it now, and he and Kevin are hoisted up together, although not before they hit a few waves. In the helicopter, both men are given blankets and checked out more thoroughly. (The life-raft and high line are picked up four minutes later by the Rosslare RNLI.)

The crew notices that Kevin is very quiet, while Ken is full of chat; he wants to take out his mobile phone and ring people to tell them he's okay. Keith puts Kevin on a special 'pro pack' monitor, which takes heart, oxygen and blood-level readings. Suddenly, Mark McDermott flicks on his landing light and right there in front of them is an unforgettable sight: just 100 yards away, the boat is disappearing before their eyes. Keith looks down at the FLIR, which is still recording, and manages to get the camera focussed on the *Renegade*. They capture the last twenty seconds as the ship disappears underneath the waves, pictures that will later appear on news bulletins.

It's only been eight to ten minutes since the helicopter came on scene, and now the *Renegade* is gone, completely. The crew is amazed at how it slips beneath the waves. 'A bit freaky,' says Dara, 'I don't think I've ever seen something like this happen, it went so quickly and left very little debris.'

They have performed a successful rescue, and all the crew has a deep sense of satisfaction. Each one has fulfilled his or her role and responsibility perfectly; from a professional point of view, it was a perfect rescue operation. They decide to go back to Waterford hospital so that Kevin and Ken can be assessed more thoroughly; both men are allowed home at midnight and are home in their beds by 1.00am. They say they had been out taking part in the search earlier in the day and were on their way to Howth for essential repairs when they noticed a serious amount of water coming in below-deck.

The *Renegade*, a 27m (88ft), sturdy, Dutch-built vessel was no match for the sea; it now lies in deep waters off the Irish coast.

12

Diving for Answers

Like the *Pere Charles*, the sinking of the *Honey Dew* is raising questions. Many people are wondering if it could have been hit by a container strayed from a merchant ship. Some say these trap air and don't sink to the bottom, becoming missiles in stormy weather. Phil Devitt, Harbour Master in Kinsale, thinks the theory is a real possibility:

> 'There are two possibilities: it could have been a rogue wave [not too long ago, a Spanish fishing boat was hit by such a wave and it blew out all the windows in the wheelhouse and knocked out all the electrics; the crew was very lucky to be towed back into Castletownbere], or it could have been hit by a container, which are a huge problem in the Irish Sea

and English Channel, containers that are blown off vessels that cross the Atlantic; these containers float just below the surface and it's a huge problem, in particular for timber boats. Because of the planking that's been found, it's very [possible] that it was hit by something. There's no system to get rid of these containers and they are a floating danger to navigation.'

People in these communities will be talking about the causes of the disaster for a long time to come.

*

Natalya Dyrin has arrived in Dunmore and is finding it very hard to comprehend matters.

She feels helpless.

She really thought her husband would be found by now.

She rings her mother and Andrey's mother. Both of them have been to a psychic, who has told them Andrey escaped as the boat was sinking and is somewhere on the coast. Natalya sees him in her mind's eye and talks to him. She still thinks he could be alive.

She pleads with God for a sign that her husband is still alive.

She looks out at the sea and asks why the wind is still blowing so hard.

*

It's not until Tuesday, 23 January that the *Rachel Jay*, the *Carmona* and the *Louvan* find the wreck of the *Honey Dew* on their sonars; it's 5 miles south to south-west of Mine Head and directly out from the picturesque west Waterford village of

Ardmore. Johnny Walsh drags a grappling hook along the seabed and pulls up a handrail; he knows it's from the *Honey Dew*.

As the Navy divers are hoping to dive at the *Pere Charles* the next day, the Garda Diving Unit heads for west Waterford. Sergeants John Connolly and John Bruton head the teams. Over the course of the diving operation at the *Honey Dew*, they use the Custom's vessel, *An tSuir Bhear* as their diving platform and are heavily indebted to Gerry Greenway and his colleagues; it's the first time a Custom's vessel has been used as a diving platform. It's also the first time in the history of the Gardaí that members have been involved in an operational dive at a wreck at sea using surface air supply to the divers below.

The *Honey Dew* is lying in exactly the same depth of water (35–36m/114–118ft) as the *Pere Charles*. The Gardaí have great praise for the fishermen whose persistent efforts eventually located the sunken vessel; Johnny Walsh and others also advised the Garda divers on the internal structure of the boat before the dive took place.

The divers have to deal with a strong sea swell and visibility of less than 1m (3.2ft). Sergeant John Connolly has been diving for more than twenty years and he describes the dive on the *Honey Dew* as 'tricky'. There were two big net drums on the stern of the vessel and, probably due to the impact of the boat hitting the seabed, one has become dangerously unstable.

When the divers reach the sunken vessel, they find it is almost completely over on its port side and already breaking up. The currents are strong and there are a number of doors and windows open, probably blown open by the force of the storm or the pressure of the invading water. There is an awful moment when one of the divers gets entangled in loose trawler netting, but his diving buddy manages to free him. The dive teams are in constant contact with the men above via wireless communication systems in their head-gear, and everything they do and see is being filmed and recorded. The Garda divers don't yet have a Remotely Operated Vehicle (ROV), but they manage to search the whole boat without one.

The dive continues for twelve days and the wreck is examined thoroughly. One of the most important finds was what appeared to be a lot of damage to the bow of the *Honey Dew*. Some of the observers think the damage looks like a 'big hole in the side of her', suggesting the boat was in fact hit by something, possibly a container.

The divers knew the possibility of finding any bodies was slim. Based on the testimonies of Vladimir and Viktor, they weren't expecting to find Tomasz inside. As the wheelhouse door was open, it was no surprise when they didn't find Ger either. He either got out as the boat went under or his body was washed out after he drowned. The news is no solace to Mary Bohan and Aneta Jagly and their children.

*

Back in Dunmore, the relatives of those who died on the *Pere Charles* are in high anticipation because they fully believe some, if not all, of the bodies are on board and will be found by the Navy divers during the following morning's search, on Wednesday, 24 January. Everyone is on stand-by for the bodies to be brought home: the divers are ready; the Coast Guard is set; the priests are on stand-by; the lifeboat is going to bring the bodies ashore; plans are made to keep the media well back. Relatives go over funeral arrangements and plan where they're going to bury their loved ones.

The morning dawns and the weather holds. At last, the divers start their descent.

This operation is unprecedented in Irish naval diving history as the divers are to search one wreck where it's strongly believed five bodies rest. Never before has such a situation presented itself. There's enormous pressure on the divers, who are very aware that the entire country is waiting, wondering, watching . . .

As the first pair of divers reaches the vessel, they are expecting to find one or two bodies in the wheelhouse. They find the windows are still intact, except one on the starboard side, closest to the seabed. One of the divers puts his hand in, but it's blocked by a flat-screen monitor that he can't pull out of the way. There is heavy trawler netting in the aft section and netting coming out of a bow locker, like a plume.

Suddenly, one diver gets caught with netting around his back, where he can't see it. It gets wrapped around the top valve on his emergency cylinder and if he moves in the wrong direction, it could envelop him. The gut reaction is to panic, but years of training kick in and, very coolly, he gets the camera (which is now on a pistol grip) and points it at the netting; he then follows directions from his colleagues via his helmet communications and carefully cuts himself free. The men get back to work. They pop the port holes to allow gas out and to put in cameras. The *Pere Charles* is now very awkward to assess as it is lying at an angle of over 170°; it has shifted since the last dive. The visibility is slightly better at 1m (3.2ft) and the divers can see that the gantry is underneath the hull and is being squashed down even more.

Using a bolt gun that fires a stud through metal, they shatter the glass in the windows, first in the wheelhouse then in the galley, toilet and other areas. They send in the cameras first and then, through a small hatch, squeeze in themselves.

They shimmy in and up and around, very slowly.

They are finally inside the wheelhouse. They look around carefully. To their utter amazement, there are no bodies.

There are gasps of surprise; they had been sure they would find Tom here and maybe at least one other man. The disappointment is immense, but they refocus their efforts: surely some, if not all, of the men will be in the galley. They are forced to return to the surface and the dive ends empty-handed. For the relatives, the strain of the expectation and disappointment is becoming harder and harder to bear.

The next day, they manage to get into the galley.

The galley isn't big and there are now two divers in it, feeling their way along slowly, shining their lights, recording every turn. At every second, they are expecting the darkness to reveal a face or a body.

Yet again, unbelievably, no bodies.

The men up above on the *Granuaile* can see exactly what is happening.

The divers search the galley again, and again, and again . . . they radio up: no bodies in the galley. They'll search here again tomorrow and then the next day, just in case they missed anything, but no, they're sure, none of the men is here.

They proceed to other areas, such as the toilet and the working areas. There's a small chance somebody might be trapped under the boat, but the divers feel it's unlikely and they certainly don't believe all five men could be there. They search in and around the boat, every inch around the hull, the netting, the decks. Every day the crowd waits with bated breath; every day they return with the bad news.

It is Dave McMeyler of the Coast Guard who has the awful task of briefing the families each day. They want to know what the divers can see when they are down there. Eventually it is agreed to show them the footage. So on Thursday night, twenty-five relatives gather in the Coast Guard station to see the images none of them will ever forget.

The families stare at the grainy pictures of the boat lying on its side, the registration number and name visible. People start crying. They didn't think their hearts could break any more, but now their hearts are shattering into tiny shards, piercing them.

Then the moment when the cameras go into the boat. Even though they have all been told no bodies have been found, each one looks intently at the television screen; maybe they'll see something the divers have missed, maybe they'll see their man. Jim Griffin has never seen so much distress in one room. At any moment, they feel they might see a hand, or a boot, or even a face. It's not to be. Lulu takes a slight hope from the images because of the amount of debris they show. Everything is all over the place, even in the wheelhouse, with all the debris down in one corner. Perhaps, maybe, when that can be shifted, they'll find something, someone?

It takes a few hours to view the excruciating pictures, then the tape spools to an end. Some of the relatives leave thinking, 'they could still be in there'.

On Friday and Saturday the shelter deck is searched again, along with other areas. But there are still two rooms/areas the divers can't get into: the bunk area and the engine room. They bring down a mini ROV and manoeuvre it into every area in the bunk section and the engine room.

No bodies.

Then they search around the boat again, in amongst the netting and in the vicinity of the sunken wreck. They search the area where the fish were. There are dozens of crabs here now and millions of what are known as 'skinners' – small insects, like sand-hoppers, that will eat anything. They multiply quickly and can take apart a large conger eel in the space of two hours. The 'skinners' are particularly prevalent off Hook Head.

By Saturday afternoon the divers feel they have done what they were tasked to do: they have searched the boat thoroughly, by man and by camera; the only two areas not accessed (the accommodation and engine rooms) were searched by camera.

The records of the Diving Unit of the Irish Navy show that at 4.20pm on Saturday, 27 January 2007, diving operations at the *Pere Charles* were concluded.

*

A short time later Dave McMeyler and the divers return to Dunmore and meet the families in the Ocean Hotel. Dave tells them the news: there are no bodies in the wreck. Slowly, the assembled gathering realises that this is now an official statement.

Regarding any doubts that the men's bodies are still on board, head diver Lt Darragh Kirwan says: 'I don't think they are on board after what we did. It's highly unlikely there are five [bodies] in the accommodation. If 50 tonne of fish can be washed out . . . we searched the accommodation and engine areas with the ROV; it went in and around bunk spaces; we got into most of the engine area.'

Lt Kirwan is satisfied that the boat has been searched, but admits there is a tiny possibility a body might still be on board: 'There is nothing more we could have done; we did what we were asked to do. We were asked to search the boat for bodies; we are satisfied there are no bodies there.'

The families are in shock, unable to accept the finality of this statement. As the divers had found so few access points and had difficulty getting into the vessel, they had naturally assumed that there was no way the men could have got out. Pat Frank says:

> 'I was full sure they'd all be inside it because we got nothing out of her, we got the life boats alright the next day but they launched themselves automatically. But nothing came out from the shelter deck. There was no fish boxes, no life jackets nothing; even when they got the first dive in they saw she was lying down on the starboard door, the only access to the wheel house from the top of the shelter deck, that that was blocked and crushed in, you know even reinforced, so I was full sure that they were all inside in her there.'

Then the questions start: if they weren't inside it, when did they get out? There are two possible answers – either as the boat was sinking or they were somehow washed out by the strong currents during the two-week gap between the sinking and the dive. If they got out when the boat was on top of the water, the *Suzanna G* was over very quickly – and how come not even one of them was found that night or the following weeks? And if they were dead when they were washed out, how come not one of them came to the top at any time?

In the weeks afterwards, Pat Frank still wakes in the middle of the night and thinks the phone is going to ring, that it'll be someone from Wales telling him they've found some bodies. He doesn't know if he'll ever get a chance now to bury his brother.

As the families leave they have been left with questions that now may never be answered. It's a harsh sentence.

13

Saying Goodbye

There is so much shock and disbelief in both Dunmore and Kinsale that no bodies have been found that the Coast Guard is asked to continue searching. In all, the Dunmore East team completes thirty-three days of searching – two weeks more than would normally be done.

'We search for longer than the set international guidelines because there is always the possibility of somebody being found,' says Norman Fullam of the Coast Guard. 'In other countries they might only search for two or three days, but here it's normally up to twenty-one days. The Irish situation is different, there is a culture here where we try to recover bodies for the families, which doesn't apply in other countries. I think it's one of our national characteristics.'

If a person drowns, the body can float for up to 24 hours and then sink. But then because of the gases released in the body, it may rise to the surface on the ninth or tenth day, will go down again and may come back up after another ten days. If it is not spotted on the surface at that stage, it will descend again and probably never be found.

The shoreline searches continue for the men missing from the *Pere Charles* and the *Honey Dew* and there will be a total of 15,000 man hours clocked up in searches that range from Cork up to the Wicklow border. The total estimated cost of the overall search operations reaches €630,000 and it becomes the longest ever search in Irish maritime history.

Some personal items are recovered, but very few. On 13 January, for example, Tramore Coast Guard finds a medium-sized T-shirt at Kilfarrissy Beach, with a logo on it that reads: 'Absolutely No Adult Supervision!' It is believed to have come from the *Honey Dew*. That afternoon a pair of size 9 runners and a wellington boot are recovered. On 15 January fish boxes from the *Honey Dew* are found. On 16 January two dark blue towels are found and three blue fishing gloves. On 20 January a blue baseball hat with the logo 'X rated' is found on Clonea beach. A fishing cap is found a few days later. Searches continue from Bunmahon until 18 February.

Jim Griffin and his colleagues had been expecting at least one of the bodies to turn up on the Welsh coast. The body of Paddy McCabe, who was lost from the *Boyne Harvester*, was found by somebody out walking in Morecambe Bay, in Wales, twenty-seven days after he went missing off Creaden Head, near Dunmore. His body had been taken all the way across from Ireland to Wales by the currents. So it was a fair expectation, but none of the seven missing men has turned up on the Welsh coast.

Slowly, the families begin to let go of hope, which is, of course, the only way lives can be rebuilt and lived again. It's part of the grieving process when the sea takes and does not return. Part of this is the awful moment when the families of the missing men are taken out to the wreck sites to leave flowers, and to say goodbye.

Lulu is dreading this expedition. She decides not to take her daughters; it will be too upsetting for them. She might take them out later in the summer, but not now, not today. Tom brought her and the two girls out for a spin in the boat two summers ago and she enjoyed it, but she's dreading the idea of climbing into the lifeboat, of being in the place where her fiancée went down with his boat. But she knows she has to do it all the same.

She arrives at the pier and meets Tom's brother, Tony, and the tears flow. Tony takes her under his arm and brings her down onto the lifeboat.

'There I am, bawling my eyes out,' she remembers, 'and every time I look out the window, I could see the different families coming down and I just couldn't believe this was happening.'

When they head out to sea it's very choppy; Lulu is amazed at the difference between the calmness of the pier and how the sea is just a few miles beyond it, amazed at how much the boat is rocking. Eventually they reach the site and the engines are turned off. The boat rocks even more. Prayers are said, prayers Lulu can't hear because she's crying so hard. They throw out the bouquets of flowers. Tom's youngest brother, Dan, throws out a box of Carrolls, the cigarettes Tom smoked. The symbol brings more tears. People are weeping over the side of the lifeboats, their salty tears dropping into the waves. The mourners look at the flowers and are struck by how quickly the wreaths disperse in different directions within only a few minutes. Lulu thinks, 'If it takes just a few minutes to disperse these wreaths, God only knows what happened to the men if they had got out; if they could go that quickly and the way they were going in different directions . . .'

For at least a month after the tragedy, Lulu's four-year-old daughter Jane thinks her Daddy is coming home. Her older sister Christine has cried every day. The first day back at school for Christine, she meets her classmate Treasa, Sarah Maher's daughter. Both have lost their fathers. Both are only five years of age. 'We're the same now, Christine,' says Treasa, 'I'll mind you and you mind me.'

Forevermore, when they smell diesel, they will be reminded of the smell of their fathers' workclothes.

For all those who were involved in the search, particularly the Coast Guard officers who were on the 'front line', it's a terrible moment when wreaths are placed at sea and no bodies have been recovered. It is a way of bidding adieu, but it's a poor substitute for having a body to bury, a grave to visit. They all feel the families' pain keenly.

'You have a feeling that you've let somebody down,' says Jim Griffin, who spent fourteen hours searching each day for many of those thirty-three days. 'You apologise to the families that there wasn't any more you could've done. You know they don't even want you to say that, but you feel like you've got to say it. You know yourself you've done your best, everybody did their best. Hand on my heart, we couldn't have done any more.'

*

It is now four weeks since the *Pere Charles* sank and all 500 tickets for the fundraiser are sold out. The Forum in Waterford City is going to experience a night like no other. Some front-row seats have been reserved for the relatives of the missing men. The relatives are in awe at the quality of singing talent of the men from Dunmore, such as master boat-builder Tony McLoughlin, Conor O'Neill, the Good Ol' Boys, Gerry Power, Tom Kelly and Martyn Simpson. Geoff Harris from Waterford Local Radio and David O'Brien have managed to get three major artists here tonight – Tommy Fleming, Finbar Furey and Phil Coulter. All three men agreed immediately when they were invited to participate.

The quality of music coupled with the show of solidarity makes the night unforgettable. Ciaran O'Neill of The Forum says that with charity functions such as this, normally some performers or backstage people ask for expenses, but tonight, not a single cent is sought; everybody happily provides their services for free.

The men from Dunmore are followed by Tommy Fleming, whose voice soars. Then Finbar Furey sings 'The Lonesome Boatman' so beautifully, it has hundreds in tears. Phil Coulter takes his place at the grand piano as the men from RNLI stations along the Celtic seaboard walk on stage. Many are wearing full emergency gear; all have been waiting for nearly four hours for this moment. Without prompting, the entire audience rises to its feet and gives the men and women of the RNLI a standing ovation; people are weeping freely all over the auditorium. Some RNLI volunteers shake at the knees, such is the wave of emotion coming from the audience. Yes, we are the men and women who go out in all sorts of conditions to rescue people or look for bodies. And yes, sometimes we think people don't really understand, but this is just unreal. Yes, we have never been appreciated and have never been so proud. As the clapping slowly stops, Phil Coulter introduces 'Home From the Sea' and even people who can't sing try. Julia and Lulu think that if Tom and Pat only knew that Phil Coulter, Tommy Fleming and Finbar Furey were playing a concert on their behalf, they'd laugh with embarrassment.

*

Friday night, 9 February, feels very cold; the howling wind makes it seem a lot colder than the 5° Celcius showing on the car thermometers as people arrive at Killea Church, just up from Dunmore, for the first memorial Mass. Seven candles are on the small table halfway up the church, waiting to be lit during the offertory procession: a candle for each man, a flame for each soul. Lulu, dressed in black, walks up the aisle with her two little girls, one holding each hand. The children's red and pink coats stand out from the dominant black. On the table beside the altar is a fish net, flowers, candles, a model of a boat and a glass frame containing a poem and the pictures of the seven men. Senior Gardaí are here, RNLI and Coast Guard volunteers. Bishop William Lee concelebrates the Mass with Fr Brian Power and Fr Robbie Grant. 'Christ Be Beside Me' is the opening hymn, and 'The Lord is My Shepherd' is sung at the end. Fr Power gives the Homily, in which he says the following:

> 'We gather this evening to remember, pray and support. To commend to the Lord the souls of those lost at sea – Billy O'Connor, Pat Hennessy, Tomas Hennessy, Pat Coady, Andrey Dyrin, Ger Bohan Tomasz Jagly – and also to offer our prayers and support to the families. We can only imagine what it's been like for you, what you've gone through; the anguish, the waiting, the longing for some

word of hope. Only those who have gone through something similar can understand what you have gone through. It's very difficult to have closure without the bodies. It adds to the pain. As a community, we share your grief. This is a tragedy which has affected not just Dunmore or Kinsale, but the whole of the south coast, all the way to the Magharees in Kerry. Those who live close to the sea know of the beauty and benefits of it. But we also know of the storms, the ugliness, the tragedies, the perils. With all the advances in navigation, safety equipment, those who go to sea are still at the mercy of the wind and the sea.'

The silence is broken by a child with a little cry and the words: 'I want my Daddy to be here'. The child is comforted, held tight and told quietly to hush now, hush . . .

*

A memorial service is held in St John the Baptist church in Kinsale at 3.00pm on 10 February for Ger Bohan. Mary wants it to be a celebration of his life because it's his birthday. The front page of the misselete shows a picture from the Bible of two fishermen pulling in their nets in a small boat, with the nets full of fish. The men are working hard.

Mary has bought a birthday card for each of the children to give to their Dad. That morning, she sends them all to their rooms to write their own personal message; she tells them to seal it, saying nobody else was going to see it. She says that after Mass, they'll post the cards. The children are baffled.

The day is damp, moist and grey and a little drizzle falls on the people as they walk up to the church. The church is packed, and many have to stand outside. Mary shepherds her four children in ahead of her and they take their seats. The church has three white balconies, somewhat like an American colonial courtroom, only much bigger. At the altar is a 'shrine' to Ger and Tomasz. Aneta, Voitek, Alexandria and their relations are here; they will have another Mass in Polish in a few weeks time. Mary's youngest child, Joseph, clings to his brown teddy.

Fr Myles McSweeney beckons the Bohans. Joseph goes up first and puts the teddy beside a picture of his Dad; Sally Jean brings up a small mermaid figurine; Mary brings a set of Rosary beads. At this stage, most of the congregation is already in tears. Reporters and cameramen are crying. 'You're working at this, aren't you?' said a member of the congregation to a reporter, 'you shouldn't really be crying.'

'I know,' said the reporter, 'but I can't help it.'

Anthony Bohan reads the first reading, from the Book of Sirach, from the Old Testament:

> 'There is a time for everything, and a season for every activity under heaven: a time to be born and a time to die, a time to plant and a time to uproot, a time to tear down and a time to build, a time to weep and a time to laugh, a time to mourn and a time to dance, a time to embrace and a time to refrain, a time to search and a time to give up, a time to keep and a time to throw away, a time to tear and a time to mend, a time to be silent, a time to speak and a time to love. All that God does is apt for its time.
>
> This is the word of the Lord.

The choir sings 'On Eagle's Wings' and the reading from the Gospel is the story of Jesus walking on water.

Fr McSweeney gives the homily, saying the gathering is a tribute and a testament to the love people felt for Ger. He says many questions remain and there are no satisfying answers, but the memories of Ger bring smiles to those who knew him. He says Ger and Tomasz were not alone that night because Jesus was there with them. Just before the Mass ends, Mary gets up to read her Communion Reflection:

> 'Death is nothing at all,
> I have only slipped away into the next room.
> I am I, and you are you.
> Whatever we were to each other, that we still are.
> Call me by my old familiar name, speak to me in the
>   easy way you always did.
> Put no difference in your tone, wear no forced air of
>   sorrow.
> Laugh as we always laughed at the little jokes we
>   enjoyed together.
> Pray, smile, think of me, pray for me.
> Let my name be ever the household name it always was.
> Let it be spoken without effect, without a shadow on it.
> Life means all that it ever meant.
> It is the same as it ever was; there is unbroken
>   continuity.
> Why should I be out of mind because I am out of sight?
> I am waiting for you, for an interval, somewhere very
>   near, just around the corner.
> All is well.'

Johnny Walsh gets up to speak and says that for Ger, Mary and his children were his life; fishing and the sea were his second love. He tells of how Ger followed his dream and bought his own boat, and then the *Honey Dew*. Many cry as he tells of how Ger was so proud of the *Honey Dew*; of how he had some bad luck with her in the past, but had always pulled through. Johnny thanks all the people who took part in the searches, saying Ger would have done the same for the same, had things been different.

The lifeboat crew from Courtmacsherry, led by Michael Hurley, then sing 'Home From the Sea'.

After Mass, Mary and the children go quietly to the pier; each with their birthday card. They huddle together, a family united and yet without their father. This is their special, private way of saying hello and goodbye. One by one they drop the cards in the water – this is their postbox.

Over the next few months, the worst for Mary is 'the fact that Ger went out the harbour and never came back in'. Mary has no body and therefore is always wondering and waiting. 'You know what is happening in your head but your heart doesn't, or vice versa, there is no connection between the two,' she says.

Mary isn't angry at the sea. 'Do I let my children into it? Of course I do; we were reared by the sea. But we were robbed . . . robbed of Ger . . . the children have been robbed of their father . . . if someone has a car accident, you have a body and a funeral . . . now it's ongoing and ongoing.'

The pain is terrible.

Ger's daughter, Sally Jean, tries to remember the happy times: the times when Dad would come in and give them all big sloppy kisses; or Christmas just gone, when James got a new bicycle and Dad tried to sit up on it and did a wheelie and landed in a heap on his back and they all nearly cried laughing; Dad wearing the silly hats from the Christmas crackers. She finds it very tough now, but anytime she feels sad, she thinks of how her Dad is here with her.

Anthony, who is in the middle of his Leaving Cert. studies, also tries to remember the happy moments: 'You'd always hear him before you'd see him; he'd roar the house down in a good way; he was great for water fights; mess fighting. It never crossed my mind that he wouldn't return; the last time I saw him was when I was sitting at the computer the day before and he was going out the door and he gave me a little joke tap on the head, said it was an accident. "Good luck, see you later," I said, presuming I would, that he'd be gone for a couple of days and then back as normal. When I first heard about the boat missing, I thought he's probably in the life-raft trying to knock a bit of *craic* out of the lads. I wasn't too worried at first, but then we got worried. The big thing is that we never got to say a proper goodbye; that is extremely aggravating; it was just so sudden. And the fact of not having a funeral doesn't help at all. Sometimes, you'd kind of still wonder will he still pop in the door, but we know he won't. We have ourselves and we have to be there for one another.'

The children still have the diaries Mary bought them after the tragedy. She told them to write down their feelings and thoughts, as a coping mechanism. One of the things Sally Jean wrote down was: 'Five steps to take when one of your parents dies'. It was practical advice; the last line reads: 'get lots of sleep'.

*

For Rose Coady, it's been a living nightmare. She can't stop thinking about her little boy, taken from her at the age of twenty-seven. She thinks about how he was a cross child for the first six months of his life; of how he was always up to all sorts of devilment; of how he never asked for pocket money, but got money from Mustard and Cruise O'Brien for helping them bring animals to the mart at weekends; of how he got on so well and looked after his sister, Carmel, who was three years younger than him, and Kelly, who was eight years younger.

Pa was only eleven when his father left for Newlyn. He was now the man of the house. Rose remembers the very day when he told her he was going to give up school and go to fish. He was sixteen at the time and while he didn't really like school, he was drawn to the sea. Rose was in Waterford Regional Hospital at the time and he walked up to her and said, 'Hey, Ma, you'll never guess what happened today?'

'What happened today?'

'I was offered two jobs and I don't know what to do.'

'What do you mean you were offered two jobs, Pa?'

'I was offered fishing and the other plastering, with Brian Clooney from over the back road. Ma, what do you think I should do?'

'Patrick, love, it's hard enough to get you to school now and everything else, sure do whatever you think yourself. You know.'

'Well, if I went plastering, I'd have a trade, but then, I'd like the fishing Mammy, I like the fishing.'

'Well, I'll tell you then, try the fishing and if it's not working out for you, go do the plastering.'

So Pa Coady started on the herrings and he rang his mother every evening as soon as the boat got back into phone range.

Kelly remembers that once he started fishing, he didn't ever want to leave it. She remembers how kind he was to her in that she never wanted for anything; with her father away in Newlyn, it was her brother who supported her when she was growing up. And then after Carmel had Shauna and Kelly had Killian, he had treated his niece and nephew as if they were his own children. Kelly repaid his many kindnesses by tidying up his flat; one week she spent two whole days tidying his flat.

Even when Rose and Steve had got divorced and he went to Newlyn, Rose knew her son wanted to help look after her and his two sisters. It was financially tough for them, but they somehow got through. And Pa had his fair share of knocks, like the time when he was a small eleven-year-old and he came home from school one day utterly disappointed. He had been told that he was 'a right little hurler but the only thing about it is that he's not a big farmer'.

For Rose, now, the worst of it is not knowing: 'I know he's with his Daddy, I know he's with his granddad, but the worst of it is not actually being able to see him, to be able to say goodbye to him. That is the worst of it. Not knowing where he is. It's just an ache, and not an ache either. It's nothing you can put your hand on. To know your son is someplace and you can't find him. To know he's there, you know, you're a mother and you should be able to look after him . . .'

And the tears flow, again and again and again.

For Rose, it doesn't matter why the boat sank. At first, she was not interested in having the boat raised: 'Patrick went that way, we know he's gone, let him rest down there.'

The lack of a grave is horrendous. Rose finds that her and Carmel and Kelly are the lucky ones in all this, for the simple reason that they believe that Patrick is with Stephen and his grandfather. They go down now to the grave in Rathdangan and light a candle there. Grandfather and Stephen are in the same grave. In their hearts, Pa is there, too.

*

Ger Bohan's best friend, Johnny Walsh, can't even begin to put his feelings into words: 'I was in Dunmore last Monday and there was a white van coming towards me and I was expecting to see Ger driving the van. It's happened to me a few times on the pier in Kinsale as well and that's the way it is, it's not final. His number is on my phone and I don't think it will ever be erased. I've telexes in the machine in the boat still from him in the log.'

*

Andrey's wife, Natalya, is planning to stay in Ireland. Natalya wants to settle here because she feels the people are very nice and it's where her husband still is. She knows he loved it here and when she sees the sea, it reminds her of him. So it's not as hard for her if she lives here with her daughter. She has to keep living and raise a child; all she can do is hope.

*

Treasa didn't believe her Mammy at first when she told her about her Daddy, but then after a while she started crying and didn't want to talk about it. She sometimes asks strange questions and is worried about her Mammy crashing the car, worried about losing her. When she says her prayers every night, she prays that her Daddy is found, or that God will find his mobile phone so he can give her a ring.

The day they go out to leave the flowers at the wreck site,

Treasa is fantastic. She brings out a letter and a picture she did at Mass, when she asked her Mammy, 'how do you spell "sink"?' In the letter, she tells her Daddy that she misses him. Out at the site, they drop the flowers in the water.

*

Even now, Sarah says, it seems unreal. Some nights she gets text messages and she thinks they are being sent from Coady; on Valentine's Day she texted him to tell him her sister had received a surprise package. The phone is still diverting to the message-minder. The evenings are especially tough and many songs on the radio remind her of him, particularly Bruce Springsteen and Christy Moore.

On the Sunday morning after Ireland beat England 43-13 in the rugby in Croke Park, Sarah and Treasa go down to the Memorial Wall to see the names that have just been added: thirteen names. Then they go for a walk on the high wall. Treasa talks about Daddy; she asks him to blow the Irish flag she is holding aloft; at that moment, the wind picks up and it blows the flag; she asks him to blow it harder, and it does.

'Look, Mammy, Daddy did that for me.'

Even at night, she blows him a kiss before she goes to sleep and catches one from him, and says she'll save it . . . she tells him he is her brightest star.

*

Mary O'Connor is still waiting for her phone to ring, for Billy to be on the other end. She can never eat another herring.

Her first ever day out at sea is to drop flowers at the location where the boat sank, where her husband last saw daylight. She can't believe how long it takes to get out the few miles from Dunmore to the dreaded place; any time she looks out from the wall in Dunmore, she thinks it's closer. She feels sick going out.

For the next few months, she will leave all the sympathy cards on her kitchen table, until they raise the *Pere Charles*.

*

Like Natalya Dyrin, Aneta Jagly wants to stay in Ireland because her Tomasz is here. He never wanted to go back to Poland, he wanted to make his home here, so this is where Aneta wants to be, close to where he is. She and Mary can't thank the people of Kinsale enough for their generosity and support. People whom Aneta never met before came up to the house and dropped in envelopes with money inside; many people came with food; eight weeks after the accident and longer, people were still calling. Some will never stop caring. Tragedy doesn't recognise nationality and the people in Kinsale have looked on these visitors as one of their own, the spirit of human bonding overcoming cultural difference.

As twenty-first-century economic migrants, Aneta and Tomasz dreamt of a better life: labour following capital, love following hope, hope for a life away from the fear of poverty, and now victims of a capitalistic society and its bank loans and EU rules and regulations.

Aneta tries hard to remember the jokes Tomasz used to tell; he was great at telling jokes and she loved the way he made her laugh. He had so many jokes in his head, all the time, so many that she wasn't able to remember them; and now, all she wants to remember is him smiling because she was smiling.

She has questioned many times the accounts of the *Honey Dew* tragedy. She couldn't understand how Ger and Tomasz, such big, strong men, were lost while Vladimir and Viktor, lithe and small, survived. She thinks of the strength of her late husband. She can see him now in the sitting room, lifting up the two children at the same time, twirling them round, holding them close. And then he lifts her up, and the children shout and whoop with joy. They were married for thirteen years, but every day was better than the last. She remembers their wedding day, the big wedding in the church, all their friends and relatives there. She was only eighteen, him only a year older. It was such a special day.

Romance was the marrow in her husband's bones. He brought her flowers more times than he got paid, kept bringing them home for her, every week, every month, every year. She knows there are not many men like that. And if it wasn't a bunch of flowers, it was a bucket of flowers. And if not flowers, little rings, jewellery, chocolates. She was always saying he brought her chocolates to make her fat; he laughs. Now, she can't take a sweet from a box of chocolates without thinking of him.

She remembers the lovely aroma of his personal smell; the smell she tries to reclaim as she puts his jumper and T-shirt to her nose; the smell that brings a unique combination of smiles and tears. There have been so many tears, too many tears. Her face is now sad. She knows she will never get over this, but she has to learn to go on, somehow. It's what Tomasz would have wanted. He wants her to smile, but it's so hard to smile without him.

*

The Memorial Service on the quay in Dunmore in March 2007 is the most emotional ever. It is the day when people claimed by the sea off this coast in the past year-and-a-half are carved into the marble. Thirteen names. Thirteen names. Thirteen names, including those who died in the *Rising Sun* and *Maggie B* tragedies.

'Never did I think in one year that we'd put so many names onto this memorial,' says John Walsh.

People came from all over Ireland to stand in tribute, to think their lonely thoughts and to dwell on what has happened and on what might have been. At least 700 people are here. This time, new faces are present, from Kinsale, Ballycotton, Cork, Offaly, Kerry, Louth; relatives who lovingly touch the newly inscribed names as if touching a coffin or a cemetery headstone; children lifted up so they can kiss the names.

The dark clouds and heavy showers threaten again, but just before 3.00pm it breaks and a weak sun appears. Prayers are recited; the expressions of stony-faced fishermen show them struggling to keep their emotions in check; many succumb and weep. The wind carries the strains of 'Ave Maria' and 'Abide With Me' out over the harbour area, towards the sea.

As local journalist John O'Connor says: 'Even though years will pass and the vicissitudes of life will change the circumstances of the bereaved, the departed will never be forgotten and will be loved forever by their spouses and partners. But it is the children and their other close relatives who will ensure that the legacies of those who were lost are kept alive on this earth. In the complex mystery and miracle of life, these children's features, smiles, mannerisms, humour and talents are safely stored in the living bodies that carry the genes and DNA of those who were taken by the sea.'

*

In that spot under the sea, 6 miles from the Waterford coast, the *Honey Dew II* continues to break up, its wooden planks shifting and tearing and tumbling away in the current. Some personal items continue to leave the seabed and are carried to beaches or rocky crevices: a pair of runners with the laces tied, a red jumper plucked out of the water by Coast Guard volunteers. Every now and then, reminders of what has been lost.

In 'The Lifeboat Inn' in Courtmacsherry, a Damien Dempsey CD is playing. At the bar, some men sit over their pints. On the walls, sketches of the *Lusitania*; the men who rowed the lifeboat from this tiny village through raging seas were the first ones at the scene. Gary Barrett is serving behind the bar. He is originally from Rush, in Co. Dublin, and has worked in the pub trade all his life. He joined the RNLI when he came here, after friends of his were drowned at sea. It takes a year to become a full member, after completing courses on first aid, seamanship, survival at sea and general emergency procedures. Ninety per cent of the training and call-outs are in fine weather; it's the extreme 10 per cent that can cause the real problems. The example set by the *Lusitania* rescuers is what Gary and his colleagues try to live up to.

'It's fulfilling,' he says. 'It's nice to be able to make a difference. And we do make a difference. I think people recognise that, like the look on people's faces when we came on to do that song with Phil Coulter in Waterford; there was pride, there were tears flowing; it was the same at the memorial service in Kinsale. It nearly broke our hearts looking at the poor people who had lost loved ones because in the mind of every lifeboat person, we all want to help.'

Gary has been in the water before, in an accident off Skerries: 'You just freeze; you see yourself going over; it happens in slow motion; you hit the water; I've been lucky enough, always wore my lifejacket; automatic inflation, then you come up, your head comes together and you think, "Ok, what do I do now?" I can't imagine what the men went through on the *Pere Charles* and the *Honey Dew* . . .'

Jack comes into the bar, a man who has spent a lot of time in the lifeboat. Time ticks slowly as another old timer sips his pint and shakes his head sadly; tragedy has been on tap here for generations. Jack has been overboard once or twice, but he has survived; he speaks softly, quietly:

> 'It's very hard on the families when the bodies aren't found. Around the coast, this coast in particular, it's after happening too many times. Other people don't understand these things. It's grand to go to a graveyard and see the headstone and say a prayer, but when the body isn't found, there's nothing there, no grave to go to. And what are people supposed to do? It's like they're in a state of limbo, there's no closure, like. You might think I'm crazy, but we believe in a kind of thing down here in west Cork . . . we believe it's a dangerous coast. I think there is some curse down around that coast, how many boats have been lost on the south coast down through the years? Some people won't fish that coast, yes, that one, from Ardmore in west Waterford to the Hook in Wexford, it's a strange coast.'

PART IV

AN INDUSTRY AT SEA

14

Understanding the Crests and Troughs

While it is important to record the facts of a story such as this, it is also necessary to reach a deeper understanding of all the elements of that story. As a writer, I felt I had a responsibility to my subject that extended beyond research and reporting; I wanted to fully embrace the daily life of a fisherman. To that end, I decided to join a fishing expedition on the *Suzanna G*, with Denis Harding. I was nervous, I will be honest, but in the end this was the only way I could get a true insight into the lifestyle of the fishermen I was writing about, and into the pros and cons of the industry in which they work. This, then, is the story of my days on the sea.

*

'See you down at the quay at 4.00, that okay?' says Denis on the phone.

'4.00am? Em, yeah, no problem. I'll be there, and I'll bring the wellies and some clothes. Do I need anything else?'

'No, that'll be grand. I have oilskins and gloves for you. Oh, you might want to get some sea-sickness tablets. See you at four.'

It's 4.00am.

The moon is full, but still struggling to penetrate the gloom. I ease the car up from Passage East to Crooke, and onwards through Woodstown towards Dunmore. Across the estuary to the left is Co. Wexford and the Hook peninsula. It was to this place that Oliver Cromwell brought his army over 300 years ago. He is supposed to have said the immortal line that he would take Waterford 'by Hook or by Crooke'.

Denis had hoped to go fishing at midnight, but the north-easterly wind that had cut down through the Irish Channel and whisked up the Celtic Sea for the last two days was still blowing hard. Denis reckons that if we head out from Dunmore after 4.00am, the wind should be starting to ease off.

'Should be?'

'Yeah, it'll probably be a bit rough out there for a while, but it'll settle down.'

How rough is 'a bit rough', I wonder.

'Just one last thing, Denis, what's this thing about a north-easterly wind?'

'It's a wind that comes from the north-east and seems to funnel down between Ireland and Wales and we get it fairly off the south-east coast. We call it a hungry wind, a lazy wind – the type of wind that, instead of going around you, it goes right through you.'

Great.

*

The car rises to the top of Killea, the hill overlooking Dunmore and the Waterford estuary where 'the three sisters' – the rivers Barrow, the Nore and the Suir – meet and flow together into the sea. On the right, an old church built in the twelfth century and dedicated to St Aodh, now in ruins. Around it, headstones of the long dead lean and bow at strange angles, weighted down by centuries of grief and neglect. Across the road, below Aggie Hayes' thatched pub, new graves cluster around the Catholic church of The Holy Cross. One headstone is dedicated to those who have no graves, to those who are truly lost at sea.

I head down the hill towards Dunmore, which takes its name from the Iron Age fort built overlooking the sea at Shanoon, a scraggy headland. The fort was built at a point known for centuries as 'Black Nobb'. An old pilot-station stands there now, precariously; a cave runs beneath it. It was on Shanoon that the first fort was built by a people who learned quickly how to defend themselves from the land and from the sea. Dunmore is now a small, touristy village in the Barony of Gaultier. There are not many places left in Ireland that use the term 'barony' to define an area. 'Gaultier' derives from the Irish 'Gall Tir', meaning 'the land of the foreigner', a reference to the large numbers of Normans who settled here from the twelfth century onwards.

Down below, the elegant granite lighthouse at the end of the pier, built nearly 200 years ago, blinks out its silent warning. The construction of the pier provided a sheltered harbour, which meant that Dunmore gradually became an important fishing port. It now boasts the second-highest figure for fish landings in Ireland, after Killybegs in Donegal. Dunmore has its own history of the sea, being the place where the first Irish woman qualified for a skipper's ticket in fishing, where the first official woman crew member joined an RNLI lifeboat, and also the place of the world record-holder for the largest tuna caught on a rod. Times have changed though and what is now left of the fishing industry is under threat: in a bid to protect fish stocks, the government and the EU continue to restrict the amount of fish that can be caught.

There's nobody around as I drive through Dunmore. Suddenly two hooded shadows dart across, bags over their shoulders, heading towards the quay. 'What a mad hour to be going to work,' I think to myself, then remember I'm on the same mission.

Turn left down to the quay as a lorry trundles up, heading away to a morning market. The words EAT MORE FISH are emblazoned on its side: a command or a plea? Shanoon rises up high to my right; on my left, the Memorial Wall.

Along the quay are the Harbour Master's office, the fish auction hall, the RNLI building, the fishermen's co-op and the ice-house. After the emptiness of the village, the bustling quay comes as a surprise: at least twenty men in overalls are hard at work, some loading gear and provisions onto boats, others driving forklifts, more clambering out of engine rooms as they wipe lubricating oil off their hands.

There's no turning back now. I park the car and take out with the wellies and bag. I need to find the *Suzanna G*: 22m (*c.* 70ft long), with the registration number W253. There are ten big boats in the harbour: some from Dunmore, others from Greencastle in Donegal, Howth in Dublin, Dingle in Kerry, Union Hall and Kinsale in Cork, and a few others from France. Some smaller boats are hoisted up on the quay, balanced between planks and tyres, ready to be repainted. Rows of lobster pots are stacked neatly along the quay wall. I notice two men about to long-jump onto one of the big boats.

'Excuse me, do you know where the *Suzanna G* is please?'

They pause, think for a second. Have they understood? Are they from Eastern Europe and struggling to understand my accent?

'Eh, *Suzanna*? Over there.'

Thirty yards away is a boat with a blue hull and a yellow-and-white wheelhouse and a wooden plaque nailed to its front proclaiming the word *Suzanna*. A silver-haired man in a grey T-shirt and blue dungarees emerges onto the wooden deck and gestures to me to come on board. I jump over and follow the man around the side and into the galley, which is the combined kitchen and eating area. There's a sink on the left, a kettle, a small cooker with bars around the top to stop pots falling over, a washing machine, microwave, worktop and fridge. The wood-panelled walls are ruby red and cream. On the right is a small red table with black plastic, anti-slip table mats. There are five holes cut into the table, into which five big mugs fit snugly, and on two sides of the table is a bench under which food can be stored. On the window-sill beside the toaster are loose cassette tapes with Lithuanian and Russian names inscribed on them; there is one tape in English: *Kylie's Greatest Hits*.

Denis appears from the far end. He's a man of medium height, well-built and he smiles a lot. He has a full head of dark hair and not many wrinkles. He looks maybe fifty, but is actually sixty-four years of age. He has just come up from the engine room, where he was checking that everything is ready for the trip.

'You made it, good stuff, we'll be off in a while . . . have you been introduced? That's Rolandes there behind you, this is

Mindes, and Alex is outside.' You can still hear the soft Dublin accent in Denis' words.

Handshakes and hellos. Rolandes is in blue, oil-splattered overalls. He's at least 6ft 2", has a firm handshake and a tanned, stubbly, weather-beaten complexion. He could be a good-looking villain in a James Bond film. And here's Alex, who could be his accomplice: younger, taller, bigger, with pale skin and blue eyes. Mindes could be their father: smaller than the other two with a pleasant smile, grey stubble, grey hair combed to one side and kind, blue eyes.

The kettle has boiled. It's Nescafé Gold Blend for Denis and Mindes, but Rolandes and Alex prefer something a bit stronger. The instant stuff is for wimps. A packet of Lavazza Rossa Espresso coffee is taken down from the shelf. Alex puts two heaped spoons of it into his mug, two into Rolandes' mug, adds some boiled water and sugar and gives it a stir. The spoon looks as if it could stand up on its own in the mug.

'Jesus, they're not going to drink that, nobody drinks that stuff straight.'

'Yeah, that's the way they like it,' says Denis laughing.

The men might drink five cups of this dastardly concoction over the next twenty-four hours. Rolandes lights a Marlboro and Alex an L&M and they go out the galley door, sit down on some ropes, drink their treacle and contemplate life.

'Rolandes sleeps here on the boat when we're not out fishing,' says Denis. 'It's handy for him and saves him on rent. It has all the facilities for cooking and washing, and there's a shower in the toilet. Down below he has DVDs, a TV and his lap-top computer.'

Alex and Mindes have come tonight in the one car from Carrick-on-Suir, where they are renting a house. Alex is in a relationship; Mindes is married, but his wife and two sons are at home in Lithuania and he only gets to see them every three or four months. Rolandes is married as well, but his wife and children are also back in Lithuania. Thirty-six-year-old Rolandes gets home only twice a year and he works and sleeps on a boat in Ireland, trying to provide for his sons in Lithuania as best he can. Over there it would be impossible for him to earn €400 a month, but here he can earn and save that over a good fortnight. He'll get home to see them soon, hopefully, but leaving them to come back to Ireland will be tough, as always.

Denis tells me that boat-owners and skippers find it very hard in roaring Celtic Tiger Ireland to get Irish men to work on the boats. A good builder's labourer can earn €500 a week after tax and is home every night at a decent hour. A trawler crew doesn't know how much money they are going to get at the end of the week because it depends on how many and what type of fish they catch. And the crew may be out fishing for five days in a row, so there's no tucking in the children every night. Trawler men like Denis may stay out for five days, return with the catch, unload it for the auction, re-stock the boat with provisions and diesel and ice, and four hours later head out again for another five days. It's only after the second five-day trip that Denis will bring the *Suzanna* home and take maybe two or three days off – before heading out to repeat the cycle. This means a fisherman may not get to see his girlfriend, wife or children for eleven days running, which is tough for all concerned.

Fishermen are not guaranteed a weekly wage either; Denis and the crew are paid on the value of the catch. No catch, no pay. When the fish is sold, the money is made up, expenses are taken out and the remainder is distributed between the boat-owner and the crew. In most boats, the owner may get half the earnings. The other half is then divided between the men, with the skipper normally getting €2 for every €1 a crew member receives.

*

The six steps to the bunks are very steep and the only way down is to face into this little ladder and slowly creep down backwards while holding onto the railing. It is hard not to hit your head. Below is a small, oval-shaped room with a table/storage area in the middle and five 'beds'. The carpet and walls are navy blue and there are small, round portholes to let in light. The only way in or out is via the small stairs. If water came gushing *Titanic*-style, would you be able to get out? Claustrophobic and cosy aren't too far away in the dictionary.

Each bunk has a curtain, which is pulled over after you climb in. And 'in' means a space 2.1m (7ft) long and 0.8m (2.5ft) wide. When your head is on the pillow, there is only about 0.3m (1ft) between your nose and the ceiling. It's a tight fit. Each bunk has a duvet (with clean duvet cover) and a pillow (with clean pillow case), so no need for a sleeping bag. Denis' wife, Joan, washes the duvets and pillow covers every week. I leave my gear on my bunk and head back up – inevitably giving myself a clatter on the head as I do so. This sort of spatial manoeuvring is going to take some getting used to.

*

Mindes unties the ropes and jumps back on board as Denis eases *Suzanna* away from the harbour wall. Denis is sitting in the big, black seat in the wheelhouse; either side of him is an array of screens and buttons; in front of him, the throttle. It's 4.40am as

198

we slip out past the small yachts. *Suzanna* veers to the right and heads towards Hook Head. Denis pushes down on the throttle and one by one the lights of Dunmore begin to fade.

Soon we are doing 10 knots. (One knot is 15 per cent greater than a land mile, so 10 knots is faster than 10mph, but not by much.) *Suzanna* cuts through the water nicely. Denis switches on the autopilot; our destination is 30 miles south-east of Waterford. The waves start to get bigger. We have three days and two nights of fishing ahead of us, and already I'm feeling fragile from the early start. Surely there's an easier way to make money.

So far, there's no sea-sickness, which is a blessing. The tablets I didn't even think I'd need must be doing their job. Denis says sea-sickness has something to do with balance, the inner ear. When he started fishing all those years ago, he suffered sea-sickness for three years, then it just left him and now he rarely gets sick. Fishermen say people are more likely to get sick in enclosed places, maybe in their bunks or in the area at the front of the boat, where the gutting of the fish takes place. Anybody who has experienced it will tell you that it's absolutely terrible. First, you begin swallowing saliva because you feel something bad is about to happen and you want to keep it down. Then you sweat a bit, maybe shake a little, and if someone is beside you, they'll tell you how white you look all of a sudden. Your legs buckle slightly. Then suddenly, aggressively, it all just comes up, and not in a controlled way, but in a completely involuntary attack – that's the only way to describe it. The pallor of your face has now turned an interesting shade of green, which contrasts painfully with the red rims of your eyes. The sweat on your forehead is flowing over your eyebrows and into your eyes, but you can't wipe it away because you are holding onto the railings for dear life, knuckles white, wrists locked. If that weren't bad enough, sea-sickness can hit twice, three and maybe four times in the space of a few minutes.

I'm still feeling a bit strange though, a slightly delirious state that must be tablet-induced. Denis glances over and seems to know exactly what's happening.

'You might as well put your head down, it'll be a few hours before we're there,' he says.

'Okay so, if you think that's alright? See you in a while.'

In the bunk, with the curtain pulled, it's pitch dark. Upstairs, Rolandes and Alex are floating on espresso. The noise of the engine is so loud, there's no way I'm going to be able to sleep. I can't help thinking nervously: am I safe here? Of course, I tell myself, everything will be fine. Denis has forty-four years' experience as a fisherman and is a natural skipper. He won't let anything happen. At least, I think ruefully, I can't fall out: the opening is too small. It must be nearly 5.00am by now and here I am, under the waterline, on a trawler heading out to look for fish. I'm trying not to think about it, but I'm wondering what it's going to be like gutting the fish . . . will I be able to hack it? The rhythm of the waves has a soporific effect, rocking me to sleep, slowly . . . slowly . . .. slowly . . ..

BANG!

An almighty noise sounds from outside, but so loud it may as well be inside my head. I leap up in fright and, inevitably, crack my head against the ceiling. I fall back down into the bunk, dazed. Denis pulls back the curtain slightly: 'We're shooting the first net, it's only half-seven and there's not much to see, so no need to get up now, stay in bed and we'll call you later.' The curtain falls and his footsteps retreat.

I fall back into a fitful sleep, and some time later am woken by the smell of a greasy fry. I throw on an old tracksuit and head upstairs, where I am greeted by daylight and a loud, cheery 'hello'. Denis glides down effortlessly from the wheelhouse. He hasn't been to bed and won't get any sleep until late tonight, but he's bright-eyed and brimming with energy.

'Good morning, hope you slept well. Would you like some tea or coffee, and maybe some toast before the breakfast is ready? We're having a fry this morning, tomorrow we might have fishcakes.'

It's nearly 10.00am.

The net was 'shot' (put into the water) an hour ago. It took Denis four hours to get to the fishing grounds. The net will be left out for five hours, so it won't be hauled back in until 2.00pm.

Breakfast is a mound of sausages, rashers and onions sloshing around in their juices and warm grease. Alex cooked this morning; Mindes will clean up. Rolandes will do cooking later; I'll clean up. With the galley tidy, Denis brings his cup of tea back to the wheelhouse. The three lads go to bed for a while. They've been up now since 3.00am and will get maybe two hours' sleep, if they're lucky, before Denis calls them for the first haul.

The 105-tonne *Suzanna* is pushing through the water at 3 knots, towing the net behind. There are two cables, each 182m (600ft) long, extending out from the sides and down the back of the boat, to the trawl doors and the net. The net that is being dragged along the seabed is 27m (90ft) wide and 2m (6ft) high. The fish try to swim away from it, but they can't, they get tired after a while and 'fall back' into the narrowest part, known the cod-end. The size of the holes in the net is dictated by the EU's Directives, which ensure that smaller fish can get out safely.

When trawling, it's possible for cables to tear, or for nets or ropes to get caught in the propeller. If a rope gets snagged in the propeller, the engine is shut down and *Suzanna* drifts helplessly, at the mercy of the elements. If Denis is unable to manoeuvre the rope free, he has to radio another boat to come and tow him back to Dunmore.

On this trip the *Suzanna* is not fishing for prawns because there are not enough days to get to the 'prawn ground' before the auction in the fish hall back in Dunmore. The 'prawn ground' is around 55 miles south-east of Waterford, in an area known as 'the Smalls', named after the rock and lighthouse of the same name off the English coast, not far from Land's End. When the *Suzanna* is prawn fishing at 'the Smalls', a chain on the bottom front section of the net scrapes along the seabed, just under the surface, where the prawns reside. If they are disturbed, they come up and are caught in the net. Some of the King prawns can be nearly 0.2m (8 inches) long.

Today, however, Denis is hunting for whitefish, that is cod, whiting, monkfish, lemon sole, black sole, John Dory, haddock and pollack. These are all demersal fish, meaning they swim close to the seabed; pelagic fish, such as mackerel and herring, swim closer to the surface.

What a fisherman tries to do, as does any business person, is to keep costs down and make as much profit as possible. Of course, money is just one of the considerations; staying alive is equally important. As a result, luck is something about which a lot of fishermen feel strongly. The old people say the sea will take a certain number of men every year, and when it is your turn, it doesn't matter how careful you are or how many precautions you take. Stories about storms at sea are part of maritime folklore, and over the centuries a bank of superstitions has built up: 'Don't start a trip on a Friday', 'Don't whistle on a boat in its boathouse'.

Although a lot of people don't believe in such omens, every fisherman probably has his own little beliefs and rituals because anything that increases the odds of not being hit by a tempestuous storm is a good thing.

'I think Scotch men are not allowed to mention pigs, white-handled knives and red-haired women,' says Denis, adding that, although he's not superstitious, he was given a special gift by an aunt years ago that has become something of a talisman. His aunt had just given birth to a fine healthy baby, and there was a fine layer of skin on the baby, known as the 'caul'. The doctor cut it off and gave it to her. She gave it to Denis because she had heard it would bring him good luck and keep him safe at sea. He still has it.

Fishing is not just about luck, if there is such a thing, it's about how a boat reacts to different situations out at sea. 'You get a feeling from each boat,' says Denis, 'it's the way a boat rolls. You get a feeling in your legs the way a boat performs, and you get used to the way your boat rolls. If you have weight in a boat, she can do something differently and you'll feel it straight away. A boat can get a little stiff and it can roll very quickly. If you have herrings in a boat, you can have a very slow roll.'

As for safety gear, there's a life-raft out at the front and one at the back of the wheelhouse. There are two sets of lifejackets for everybody: one for deck work weather and a chunkier one. There is a box of flares and line throwers, as well, which are used for shooting a line to another boat.

'Then we have this transponder, which sends out a signal if we get into difficulty,' says Denis, 'and the EPIRB. It costs €1,500 to service each of those life-rafts every year.'

Denis flicks through the book that shows how much he is allowed to catch this month. These figures are his quotas. In the spaces beside whiting and pollack, it says OPEN, which means he can catch as many of these species as he wants – or, more appropriately, as many as he can find. Only 5 per cent of his total catch for the month can be plaice or sole, and he's allowed to catch 5 tonnes of lyng and 3 tonnes of monk. Each fish box can take 40kg of monkfish, so this month they are allowed to catch seventy boxes of monkfish. The big money at the moment is in prawns: for small prawns, Denis will get €3.90 per kilo in the auction, but €9.50 a kilo for the bigger ones. He's allowed to catch 30 tonnes of prawns in this month alone.

When Denis returns to Dunmore in a few days time, he expects to get on average €60–€70 for a box of whitefish. Of those, a box of whiting will be worth less than any of the others. At the moment, fishermen get only €1 for a kilo of whiting; it sells in the supermarkets at €17 a kilo! But a box of prawns could fetch €110. A fisherman gets around €2.40 for a kilo of cod, €6 per kilo of John Dory, €2.20 per kilo of lemon sole and €1.80 per kilo for ray.

'Housewives probably think we are making a load of money because of the price they have to pay for fish in the shops. And many of them can't afford to buy it. Fishermen don't get that price, we get nothing near it,' says Denis.

On average, *Suzanna* has to catch €1,000 worth of fish a day just to make it worthwhile to be out here; that's €1,000 at auction prices. If a quantity of fish is bought for €1,000 in a fish hall, it'll probably be 'worth' ten times more by the time it reaches the supermarkets. Whatever price Denis gets has to cover all the costs and pay the owner's share, Denis' share and the crew's share.

It's not much for what these men have to do: life on a trawler is tough. After four or five days fishing, the crew comes back into port at maybe 7.00pm for a fish auction. While the catch is being unloaded, another crew member goes up and buys boxes of food. The boat is moved over to the ice plant, and 1.5 tonnes of crushed ice is loaded onto it. By 10.00pm, just three hours after landing, the crew is heading out for another spell at sea.

'You'd have to like it to do it,' says Denis, who tells me it is getting harder because he and others seem to be putting in longer hours than they used to years ago just to make a living wage.

*

Soon it's time to haul the net.

Denis eases back on the throttle and brings *Suzanna* round as gently as possible in the strong wind. The three men guide the section of the net known as the cod-end on board and manoeuvre it directly over the wooden 'pen', or pound, on the deck. Rolandes pulls hard on the release rope and the fish pour out into the pound with a big *whhhoommppp*.

The men shake it until all the fish are in the pound. Rolandes re-ties the rope and signals to Denis to lift away. It's taken half-an-hour to haul the net, empty the cod-end and return it to the seabed, where fishing has now resumed. The net will be left there for another five hours and the same process will take place again. So, if nothing goes wrong, every five hours it's net in, net emptied, net out. The next haul will be at 7.30pm, the next 1.00am and the next, 6.30am.

Rolandes and Alex suck on cigarettes as the sorting begins. Mendes pumps water into the fish pound. Some of the fish are still flapping, others have given up. Some are small, others big; some are ugly, others beautiful.

'None of the fish survives the journey up from the bottom,' says Denis. 'They've just come up 360 feet or 60 fathom in less than twenty minutes. It's like a diver, they get the bends. You see the different colour in their eyes, the pressure from the bottom to the top is too great for them.'

'Sometimes we might get a shark,' he continues. 'Some can be up to 30 feet long. We get the odd basking shark, but mostly they're blue sharks. We try to get them out of the net before they come on board, the feckers would eat you if they came in. A shark on the deck can do a lot of damage, especially a big one. If they're very big – anything over 15 feet long – we cut the bag in a certain way, put a strap on his tail, slack the net back down, then get the net away from it, cut the strap and leave them off back into the sea. If a shark gets on the deck, it's nearly impossible to get it out. We also get eels sometimes. They're like vicious, long, grey snakes, up to 6 feet long. They hide under the fish. If you're trying to pull out a big cod and put your hand down, the eel might see your hand and he'll go for it. He can bite right through glove and skin and even bone and could take the hand off you. Sometimes we'll get them after bad weather. We try to throw them out as carefully as possible. Some guys bring them in, but they don't usually get much for them.'

The water in the pound lifts the fish onto the rungs of a small conveyor belt and they land *schuulrppp* on the steel, semi-circular, rotating sorting table, one end of which is a chute that leads to a hole and back to the sea. The men have large plastic baskets and fish boxes down at their sides and as the fish come up, they separate them and throw them into the different boxes. Fish that are too small go out the chute and back to the sea. The raucous gannets are waiting for them; most are dead by now anyway, killed by the bends.

'It's a waste throwing them back,' says Denis, 'but you just can't have them.'

Other fish that won't sell in the auction halls are also thrown back, such as the fiercely ugly dogfish, a mucky brown-coloured, 0.5m-long (1.5ft) creature. His skin is hard, his flesh is supposedly rancid; even the gannets won't eat him. You'd want to be starving and contemplating eating your crewmates before you'd eat a dogfish. Dozens of rejected creatures are flushed down the chute and float away, belly-up. These and the small fish are the unlucky ones – unlucky to have been caught and now unwanted by man or bird, the by-products of trawling.

Once the fish have been sorted, the first basket is lifted up and the fish are emptied out onto the steel table. The flat fish are done first – lemon sole, plaice, black sole and megrim (a fish popular on Spanish tables). The men reach for their small, sharp knives, give the blades a few rubs against a handheld sharpening stone and begin gutting. The fish are cut in a certain way and the guts, intestines and innards are scooped out. Gutting is necessary to ensure fish don't go off before the boat makes it back to port; the guts of a fish deteriorate first.

The whole operation is done standing up. Rolandes shows me how to gut a flat fish by making a small incision half-an-inch under the eye, cutting across an inch and then pulling out the guts with the knife and a flick of the wrist. He makes it look very easy, but it's hard to do, especially as the boat is swaying and the lemon sole is still moving. The skin is tough (even tougher on the plaice) and what they do in four seconds takes me fifteen. The lemon sole doesn't produce too much blood.

Next up is a black sole, bigger, rarer and worth much more than its cousin. I let Rolandes gut him, given his size and worth. The gutted fish are thrown into baskets and all the guts and blood left on the table are pushed by hand (everybody's wearing gloves) down the chute and out. The pollack and cod are thrown up on the table next. When they're finished, the haddock, whiting, ling, monkfish, John Dory, ray and whatever else has been caught is gutted.

If you're not used to it, gutting a 0.8m (2.5ft) cod is a hideous, ghastly, scary and stomach-churning experience. I'm standing there, with my pathetic little penknife, and in front of me lies a fine specimen of one of the most important fish ever to have graced our oceans. Wars have been fought over this fish, books written about it; some say this fish changed the world. Now here he is, spreadeagled on the table and not in a terribly good mood. He has a grey, silvery body with a green tint. No matter what way I move, he's staring at me, like the Mona Lisa. His big mouth is open slightly, as if he's gnarling. He is dead, isn't he? What the hell do I do next?

Cod swim with their mouths open and will swallow whatever they can. It has long been prized for the whiteness of its flesh. Almost all 200 species of cod live in the cold salt waters of the Northern Hemisphere, and they have probably been around for about 120 million years. The Atlantic cod is the largest and is considered to have the whitest and tastiest meat. Studies show that seas across the world are being emptied of older fish, such is the pressure on stocks. In some areas, a plaice gets no older than six years (if allowed, it could live up to the age of forty); cod has evolved to live twenty years or more, but most rarely reach six.

Mendes picks up a cod by the mouth and turns him so his belly is facing up. With one hard, clean stroke he cuts across the neck – the place where a windpipe would be, if fish had windpipes. The trick is not to break the neck. The blood shoots out onto Mendes' oilskins; some may even have got into his hair. Without flinching, he cuts deep and long on the soft, white belly. Whereas the guts of the lemon sole could be pulled out using the head of the small knife, the guts in a cod have to be reefed out with one and maybe both hands. He pulls and tugs and rips and then cuts the last bit of intestine. I'm amazed – so much guts for one fish, it's enough to fill a medium-sized saucepan. But six, maybe seven seconds is all it takes and it's all done, fish gutted, clean, drop him into the basket, push the guts down the chute, next.

Dear God, I don't think I can do this. The cod eyes me glassily; I eye him warily. This is a battle of wills. Okay, here goes . . . I hold him down with my right hand, insert three fingers of my left hand into his mouth and hold my thumb under his 'chin'. Just as I do this, he bites me.

I nearly collapse with fright.

The cod writhes in an attempt to get away. He can't be still alive. He's been out of the water half-an-hour. He's heavy, and strong. But wait, his teeth can't get through my gloves, but they are closing tighter on my fingers. I get my right hand and pull his jaws apart. He looks at me – his life is nearly over, but he's got one more surprise for me.

I cut the neck bone slowly, as much in fear as in reverence: fear that he'll squirt blood in my eyes. There's a deep gurgling sound in response. I slide the knife into his belly, as quickly and cleanly as I can so I won't have to do it twice. Some of the guts just flow out. There's green stuff, white stuff, half a fish, black stuff, bladders, blood. And his last act of defiance? The smell. It is simply unreal, beyond description. It hits me in the face; I can nearly taste it. I close my mouth to stop myself from getting sick, but then realise I'll have to breathe through my nose, which is worse. So I try not to breath as I cut and hack and pull the guts out and finish the job. Finally, I lift him up and put him in the basket. That is the one and only cod I gut on the entire trip. I wisely leave the rest of the cod (and the equally angry-looking pollack) to the experts.

The gutted fish are put through a cleaning device, basically like a washing machine for fish. Mendes washes down the table surfaces, and within a few minutes what had looked like a mini abattoir is now sparkling again.

Rolandes opens the hatch in the middle of the deck and climbs down the ladder into the cold storage area below, where the temperature is kept at -1° Celsius. The crushed ice is kept in the two pounds to the front. These are sections, or compartments, divided by timber planks slotted one on top of each other until they nearly reach the ceiling. Food such as steaks, milk and bread are kept in another pound down here. Using a rope with two hooks, Alex lowers down the baskets of fish as Rolandes shovels ice into each box. The fish are packed by type into boxes and when a box is full, it's sprinkled with ice and pushed against the wall. The empty baskets are brought back up and when everything is in place, the hatch cover is closed.

The men take off their oilskins and boots and make coffee. It's 4.00pm. The next haul will be at 7.30pm. Dinner has to be prepared, eaten and the kitchen cleaned. There might be a little bit of time for relaxation, but not much.

It's not long before 7.30pm comes around and the entire process is repeated. This time, the catch is not as good. The nets go back down at 8.00pm and will be hauled again at 1.00am.

By 11.00pm, tiredness hits. Denis is still at the wheel; the weather shouldn't be getting worse, but it is. The *Suzanna* is now being thrown hard from side to side. There is no way that this north-easterly is going to let me sleep. For Denis, it's nothing to worry about; boats are built to survive bad weather. But for me, it's deep breathing time. The boat is moving so violently that I am being thrown around in the small bunk. Maybe it's getting up to a Force 8 or 9 out there. The noise of the wind and the waves and the engine and my heart is frightening. Surely, it can't get any worse.

*

You have to be a certain type of person to be a fisherman. A fisherman is a weather forecaster, a reader of the elements, a risk-taker, a hunter, a gatherer, a brave person, a fighter of bad conditions. Many fishermen see themselves as part of a special band of brothers who have survived many battles with the elements. I can now understand why they are a special breed. Thousands of books have been written about the sea, but it's not until you are out in a storm in the middle of the night that you get to appreciate its true ferocity. I can tell you, 30 miles from land in a storm, in the dark, is not a good place to be.

The men have already hauled and are sorting the fish. Denis is in the wheelhouse. The wind is howling so violently, I'm cursing at it in desperation. My body is aching with tiredness. It's cold, and the rain is hammering down. The boat is rolling, sliding on water as it sloshes in over the sides before escaping out the 'scuppers'. The spotlights on the boat show us each wave approaching, crashing against us with a bang and another bang and another bang. Beyond the reach of the spotlights, however, it's just black darkness. No lights from other boats; maybe they're not there. Nothing to see only waves and rain; nothing to feel only the cold, clammy wet and the nervous tension.

The waves are maybe 3m (10ft) high as I start walking up the port side, towards the front of the boat. A big wave crashes in and throws me violently, and I grip the railing tightly. The *Suzanna* and I are both leaning crazily, and I can feel the sea licking against my fingers grasping the railings: the black water is less than 1m (2ft) from my face. The water looks very, very cold. If I lean any further forward, I'm pitching in head-first. If *Suzanna* doesn't straighten up, I am about to get a dreadful soaking. The moment when I was nine years old and couldn't swim and and fell into a river while rod-fishing with my father comes back with intense clarity. I remember plummeting through the water and hitting the riverbed, 6m (20ft) below. I started kicking desperately, then up through the murky water, I could suddenly see my father's arm reaching down. He pulled me up and I coughed up water, spluttering back to life. Right now, facing this churning, salty water, I wish I was anywhere but here.

Suzanna straightens up. I walk on, or rather stumble, feeling disoriented and faintly sick. I think of my cousin, Noel Jordan from Lisdoonvarna, teaching me to waltz: lean on your left, then shift your balance to your right, get the knees to buckle at the right moment. Now here I am, waltzing with the waves, skating with the sea. A few more steps and I reach the front of the boat.

This, truly, is not a nice job; not in these conditions. People might have a bad day at the office, but a bad day at the office out here could mean the difference between living and drowning. Denis says he wouldn't stay out in a persistently bad storm, which means waves over 4m (13ft) high. He adds that it's not that the boat wouldn't be able for it, it's just that he wouldn't catch much fish. I wouldn't do it because of the sheer terror of being out here, in this, with no escape route.

For now, another nice hour of gutting beckons. The lads seem grumpier, but they're bound to be, they're worn out now and the weather is against them and the catch is the smallest one so far. Rolandes turns on his compilation tape of Russian disco music and a horrendous *thump/thump/thump* engulfs the gutting area as an octopus comes up on the conveyor belt. It's changing colour before our eyes and is probably relieved at being thrown back down the chute, such is the sound of the 'music'. There's very little talking between the men. Everyone is bleary, weary and working on autopilot.

It's hard to stand straight because the swell is so great, the waves are so high and the wind is so strong. It's 2.00am and for some bizarre reason, I'm thinking about Bruce Forsyth and 'The Generation Game', with the fish as prizes coming up on a conveyor belt. Here comes a monkfish. I never thought such a tasty fish could have such a big, humanlike head and be so shockingly ugly. Oh no, what's this? I gulp hard as a dead gannet stops in front of me. Gannets are big, white birds, bigger and nastier than seagulls. I was looking at them earlier, remarking on their speed through the air and intelligence in being able to identify, from 6m (20ft) above, the fish that was being thrown out. This one won't be doing any more swooping. It must have got caught in the net a few minutes ago, or did it die weeks ago and was picked up in the cod-end? Mendes picks it up by its neck and throws it down the chute.

After that, it's like a dream dreamt in extreme conditions. Denis says two of the lads will stay up for the next three hours while he sleeps. The autopilot has a device that emits an alarm-clock sound every three minutes in the wheelhouse. It keeps going off until you press a small red button. It's very annoying, but necessary – in case anybody falls asleep at the wheel. As I climb into my bunk, I hit my head again, inevitably. But it doesn't matter. At this stage, nothing matters. Nothing but lying down and resting. Sleep comes quickly, and kind-hearted Denis lets me sleep through the 6.30am haul.

The smell of fishcakes being cooked on the frying pan wakens me at at 9.00am. Rolandes has made gorgeous fishcakes, using 3 kilos of fresh haddock, onions and breadcrumbs. At 80 cent a kilo for haddock, the fish for this meal for five costs only €2.40; the same quantity of haddock in a supermarket would cost maybe €20. Everybody eats well and smiles at the news that the north-easterly has gone away to annoy somebody else. The difference is remarkable: everything and everybody is calm now. After his three hours of sleep, Denis is listening to Ryan Tubridy on long-wave on the radio.

The routine reasserts itself: haul, empty, shoot, sort, gut, clean, store, eat, relax, sleep, haul, empty . . . dinner, coffee, breakfast, and so on . . . thankfully, nothing goes wrong, the fishing is good, the men are in fine form and before I know it, it's time to go home.

'We all look forward to getting home,' says Denis. 'In this business, you could be at home for three hours in a fortnight. It's not your average job. You're always thinking about the people at home and how they are thinking about you. It's hard on families because you're not there, and you miss a lot of the children growing up. But I still enjoy it, I wouldn't change a thing. Is there a future in this job? Yeah, I think so, especially after the government's plan to decommission some boats. Some of the boats left should do okay. Look, there in the distance, Hook lighthouse; it's great to see it. When we see the Hook on the way out, you know you might have five days ahead of you of hard fishing. But when you see it on the way back, you know you're nearly home.'

Suzanna comes home to Dunmore on a calm, still evening. There's no auction tonight, so after tying up, the fish boxes are lifted out of the hold using a rope-and-pulley system and moved into the fish hall by one of the young lads working the forklift for the co-op. Denis will go out again in a few days time. Would you like to be a fisherman, so? he asks. Truthfully? No. And whoever thinks fishing is easy, is wrong.

When Denis passes up the quay in a few minutes time, he will drive past the Memorial Wall. 'I always say a little prayer,' he says.

15

What Caused the Disaster?

Viktor and Vladimir believe the *Honey Dew* sank after it was hit by a mammoth wave from which it couldn't recover. While there are still some questions about the loss of Ger and Tomasz. For the relatives of those lost on the *Pere Charles*, many questions remain.

Michael Walsh is still trying to figure out what happened to the boat he believed was the perfect vessel. He still doesn't know, but he is searching for the answer anywhere he can. He has, for example, been studying a book on how weather impacts on the environment:

> 'I know people say it was a fine night that night, but a container ship was struck the same week by a freak wave. I think the weather is not natural, I think the weather is not

the way it was, when you would know when every wave was coming . . . I think that maybe it was a combination of two or three things that sunk the boat . . . I don't think it was the weight of fish that sunk the boat . . . I think she took a slop of water and the fact that the fish was in her, she couldn't clear the water off herself. I don't think anything went wrong with the boat.

I can't pay a greater tribute to the men who are gone – they loved their families, their families loved them, there is no greater honour for you or me or anybody else . . . they worked hard and played hard and loved the job . . . the biggest thing that plagues me was the fact that there was so much safety gear on my boat . . . and the fact that ten of the fourteen men who have been lost here in the past eighteen months have been lost with no trace of them . . . I would like to see how can we change that to bring something practical into the fishing industry that actually saves people's lives . . .'

Like Michael Walsh, Denis Harding is condemned to play that night over and over again in his mind, looking for any small clue he might have missed in the horror of the moment. The months pass, life goes on, but he still can't fully comprehend what happened the night the *Pere Charles* sank:

'There was no distress in Tom's voice. He didn't say "Get over here quick, the boat is sinking" or anything like that. He just said, "She's broached, stand by us".

You know, I think if it was me, I'd be fucking screaming. But then maybe at that moment in time she wasn't dangerously broached, he might have thought she was going to come right, and that he wanted the *Suzanna* just to stand by anyway ... I just don't know.

What's killing me is that we couldn't get to them. To think they were so close. If they got out in a life-raft or got out and held on to anything, we'd be there for them. If he'd given any indication that she was going down, but no, there was no panic in his voice or anything. He said the words in an ordinary, conversation tone.'

Denis goes over it again and again. After the two boats separated and were heading towards Dunmore, he knows that Tom would have had everything tied down. Something went wrong very quickly, so quickly that Tom hadn't even had time to press the distress button.

What could possibly have happened in those seconds? If the *Pere Charles* had taken in water, Denis reckons that Tom wouldn't have run down to the engine room. The only reason he'd have to do this would be if one of the pumps needed to be turned on from within the engine room. However, the buttons to work the pumps on the *Pere Charles* were in the wheelhouse, the same as in the *Suzanna*.

What about a fire on the boat?

No, Denis thinks this is unlikely as Tom would have said as much when he contacted him. Tom had a small television screen in his wheelhouse showing him what was going on in the engine room, so if there had been a fire down there, or anywhere on the vessel, he would have seen it and said so. Furthermore, a fire wouldn't have caused the boat to broach.

Tom's only message was that the boat had broached. Denis believes this means that water came in on the *Pere Charles* in some way: 'She sheared away on him and he lost the steering some way; that's what broached means; you lose control in that split-second.'

The weather wasn't too bad, thinks Denis, but did the weather and the waves have some part in it? What about a rogue wave?

'A bad wave could have happened, but they weren't in far enough to be in the "race of the Hook".' And, of course, Denis was out there as well, not 2 miles from the *Pere Charles*, and the *Suzanna G* wasn't hit by anything to suggest a massive wave. That isn't to say it's impossible, though. Other fishermen have experienced a 6m (20ft) wave coming down on top of them all of a sudden, while no such wave attacks their fishing partner only a few hundred yards away.

Denis admits he wasn't close enough to Tom to see if a wave went in over the stern. If it had, what would the effect have been? Normally, it should have no effect because the water should wash off the deck through the 'scupper', the small holes on either side. The boat may be rolling from side to side, but a wave shouldn't cause it to sink.

In reality, most accidents derive from a combination of factors. So all we can do is examine the possible factors that caused the sudden catastrophic event that brought about a point of no return. The only people who could tell us what actually happened are the five men on board that night. In their absence, we will never know conclusively; we can only surmise.

The first thing we know is that the *Pere Charles* was full of herrings. The weight of 50 or 60 tonnes of herrings would have made the boat sit lower in the water, but it was a boat that was well capable of carrying such a weight. The distance between the deck of the vessel and the waterline (known as the freeboard) was reduced by the weight. When the freeboard is reduced in any boat, the handling abilities of the boat can be affected. If the herrings were distributed evenly down below between the port and starboard pounds, then the centre of gravity of the boat should not have shifted. Once the fish didn't shift or move down below, the boat should have been able to right itself as it rolled with the waves.

The first question then is: did any of the pound boards down below break or shift in any way that caused the fish to shift, which in turn would have caused a potentially serious imbalance? Michael Walsh says new pound boards and stanchions had been fitted to the boat just before Christmas, so he is ruling out that possibility.

The net was back up on the drum, so the possibility of the net being caught in the propeller is also extremely remote.

The next question is whether there were any herrings on the deck of the *Pere Charles*? Denis Harding says he couldn't see if there were, but he is certain Tom would have made sure everything was secure as he headed for Dunmore. If there were herrings on the deck, sloshing around in their own juices and water, could they have blocked the scuppers if water came in on the stern of the boat? And if they did, what effect would this have if another wave then came in, adding to the water on the deck that hadn't been able to escape?

As the *Pere Charles* was a shelter-deck boat, the only way water could have come in on the deck was at the stern. The boat was heading in a north-westerly direction and the waves were coming from a south-westerly direction, so there was no inherent danger if this course continued. Some fishermen believe that, for some reason, the boat must have 'turned' to its right-hand, or starboard, side (this must have been the 'broaching' Tom referred to) and then probably took on more water at its stern.

Another question: was the hatch to the pounds left open? Again, Denis says Tom would have ensured everything was secured and tied down. If the hatch was open and water came onto the stern of the vessel, some of it would have gone down the hatch. If that then caused the herrings to slosh around that little bit more, could it have been sufficient to have brought about a crisis of stability?

So what caused the *Pere Charles* to broach?

It's probable that Tom Hennessy was steering the boat manually and wasn't using the autopilot system.

Something happened to cause a man as experienced as Tom to lose control of the steering. Had something gone wrong in the steering compartment down below? Michael Walsh thinks not. Had he been steering manually and did some of the fish shift just as a bigger-than-normal wave hit the boat? Did Tom drop into one of the infamous troughs off Hook Head, causing the boat to lurch to the starboard side? And in this precarious state, did another wave then come in and deliver the fatal blow? Did the water get in under the shelter deck and rush up towards the bow, leading to the broaching effect?

The natural reaction for any person in charge of a vehicle, car or boat when a problem occurs is to slow down and try to solve it. If you are on a big wave, you don't speed up; you pull back on the throttle and try to get control of the situation. So if the boat was broaching, as Tom said it was, the likelihood was that he pulled back on the throttle. This would have reduced his speed, but wouldn't have cleared the water from the stern. If water had come into the stern of the boat under the shelter deck and wasn't able to clear quickly enough, the handling of the boat would have been affected. And if the fish plus whatever water was on the vessel moved too far to the one side at the same moment, the boat could literally have just toppled over and sunk.

The ability of a boat to right itself is called 'stability'.

The term Tom used, 'broached', is used by seafarers when a sea breaks into the boat. It can happen if a boat is 'running ahead of weather'. In other words, the south-westerly wind was behind Tom and slightly to the left, driving the waves onto his port side; the waves are 'up his ass' in fisherman parlance. As Denis describes it:

> 'A boat can shear away on the sea. They get up on the sea, so your rudder is no good to you. The boat won't steer. In fact, sometimes the boat can turn completely around and face the opposite way. The sea is gone from underneath the stern of the boat. Kiting is the word, maybe, or surfing. Then that wave goes away from under the boat, so there is nothing left under the boat, and the rudder doesn't steer.
>
> If something was going wrong, the first and most natural reaction would be to pull back the throttle; to stop the boat in the water and give her a chance to clear herself because the faster the boat is going through the water, the more chance she has to roll. You must slow down the boat. Slowing down the boat would get rid of the first problem, such as water on the deck, but if she listed over too badly, the next wave could break in on the boat.'

Denis has seen rogue waves that, even on a calm day, come out of nowhere and take boats completely by surprise:

> 'You'd say to yourself: where did that come from? It would slash off the side of the boat and break into the boat.

Sometimes it wouldn't do any harm, the scuppers would clear it out, but if you were steaming at 7 or 8 knots and a sea broke into the boat, it may not clear itself, and if the boat listed over for too long, another one might break in and that would be the difference between your stability and no stability. And that could do harm.'

Boats are built to a certain level of stability, but if one thing, or series of things, causes the boat to go beyond that level, it can tip like a spinning-top because there is more weight on top than there is underneath. There is not enough weight on the underside of the boat to bring it back upright in the water. It reaches that critical moment where stability is lost forever, and the boat sinks.

Fishermen in Dunmore believe 'there must have been a certain amount of sea and swell' for a powerful boat such as the *Pere Charles* to have sunk; the one thing Tom didn't have control over was the weather. If water did get onto the stern, under the shelter deck, and if the boat then fell into a trough, buoyancy could have been lost and it may have gone over on its starboard side. The fish may have begun to fall out as the boat sank.

What is known about stability is that waves cause a boat to roll from one side to the other and the positions of the Centre of Gravity and Centre of Buoyancy are constantly changing. Even a relatively small change during the rolling motion, such as cargo shifting, can create a negative righting moment, which can cause the boat to capsize in seconds.

Whatever happened, it happened extremely quickly. It wasn't totally unexpected, however, because Tom obviously knew something was going wrong, even if he didn't know what that was. Denis says there was no panic in his voice, but there was something the matter. Fishermen know each other's way, know that, in general, they can be very understated. They don't have to say there is a major problem; another fisherman will understand by what he's hearing that there is a major problem. Whatever caused it, Tom felt the need and had the time to make one radio call to Denis, but he didn't have time to make a second call. The likelihood is that when Tom made that last VHF contact, matters were probably going, or had just gone, beyond his control.

Denis can't help thinking about what the crew might have been doing in those crucial final moments. He reckons they would have been sitting down in the galley to eat because they had three or four hours of unloading ahead of them at Dunmore. Tom was definitely in the wheelhouse, at the wheel, because he spoke with Denis on the VHF. Denis didn't hear any other voices in the background during that brief message from Tom. Was somebody else in the wheelhouse with him? Coady, perhaps, chatting about the great catch?

> 'From the very second it would have started going, you'd be horsed from wherever you were sitting across to the other side; everything would start flying – if it did happen like that. You just lose your sense of direction.'

Denis wonders about time: how long was it from the moment he heard Tom's voice to the sinking? Probably 30 seconds maximum. Maybe they went down in half that time. Maybe the *Pere Charles* was going down as Tom was speaking to Denis, but Tom hadn't realised it.

Denis knows that if the *Pere Charles* was broaching, she could have turned over as she went under. The crew would have been completely disoriented. An important point to remember is that none of them would have been expecting it: they were on their way home, they had had a great day fishing, they were relaxing before reaching the quay and doing the unloading. They all would have been smiling, satisfied with their day and looking forward to seeing their families. Even if any of them were wearing a lifejacket in the galley (something that is never done), it could not have changed what happened next.

Only those who have died at sea know the full extent of the horror as it unfolds, but fishermen who have experienced close calls can give us a chilling insight into what those last moments may have been like. The men in the galley feel the boat going hard over to one side as it broaches, and steady themselves against the wall or by grabbing onto the table. Some are wearing their oilskins; some would have taken them off; most, if not all, have taken off their boots; some have put on shoes; some are wearing just socks. Their tea or coffee splashes out of the mugs. The radio on the ledge falls over, but the music continues. The boiling water and potatoes on the stove spill out of the pots; the ashtray slides across the table. All this happened very quickly, in no more than two seconds. The men who were standing (maybe Billy is at the sink, peeling vegetables) would have shifted their weight from one foot to the other in an effort to maintain balance. Everybody waits to feel the boat leaning back to level.

Instead of it coming back, the boat continues going over on its side. The next few seconds are chaos.

Everybody and everything is flung to one side in the small galley. The men's feet are lifted off the ground, their arms are outstretched as they try to stop their heads hitting the walls and the ceiling. Cups, plates, pans, books . . . everything is thrown all over the place. Some of the men shout, another curses. And then the boat starts sinking. As it does so, some are upside-down, squashed against each other, elbows in faces, knees in backs, heads jammed against a window. Some may be knocked unconscious. There's no time to make sense of it, to get to grips with the situation: it's just a few seconds of blind fear, panic and disorientation. As this confusion is happening, a torrent of water cascades up into the galley. It doesn't stop. It just keeps coming. The men, now upside-down, get a mouthful of water and try to get out of the room. They push against each other, but more and more water is coming in, forcing them back.

Up in the wheelhouse, Tom is experiencing the same horrible sensations. He is thrown against the sideboard and the equipment. Water rushes in, everything is upside-down. If he tries to stand up, he'll be standing on what was the ceiling. But the boat continues to move, to roll, causing further disorientation. That's if he is still in the wheelhouse at all. The wheelhouse door will later be found to be locked, so maybe he tried to go down towards the galley/engine to sort out whatever problem was occurring, or to warn the men? Wherever he was, he didn't have the time to reach up and press the distress button. It must all have happened so terribly quickly.

The noise is overwhelming, the sensation of being torn from the surface and thrust to the deep is petrifying.

And then the awful moment when the lights go off.

The need to live, to survive, to get out is frantic. The men push and kick and grab and flail, trying to find the door, trying to get out the door, trying to find and help one another. There are hundreds of gallons of cold, cold water flooding through and filling the rooms, so quickly. Perhaps some manage to reach the door – a glimmer of hope – but are forced back by the surging water. Perhaps a man even manages to get out, but he is already holding his breath, already needing to gasp for air, and the surface has disappeared in the inky blackness, and the force of the water and the sinking boat are pulling him down. He can't hold on. The boat is sinking, and sinking fast. All is complete darkness and utter desperation. There may be air pockets and areas where some of the men survive a little longer than others, but within a very short time every area in the boat is underwater. Instinctively, they try not to breathe underwater, refusing to inhale until they reach the verge of losing consciousness. The *Pere Charles* lands heavily on the soft seabed, sending up clouds of sand-smoke. The vessel shudders, then settles. Outside, all is silent. Inside, there may be pockets of air in which some of the men survive for a few more seconds. The door from the galley to the deck may be open. Everything is pitch black. Some may feel their way along the wall or ceiling in a hope of making it to the galley door and out and up. The thoughts of each man must be of survival and then, of their loved ones.

It has taken less than a minute for the big trawler to fall 35m (114ft) to oblivion. The net on the drum, already coming loose on the descent, has now unravelled even more and tangles itself around a section of the sunken vessel. The boat has landed on its starboard side. Its bow is facing in a northerly direction, towards Waterford, the Suir estuary and Hook Head, whose light continues to blink. Already, the currents at the bottom are sucking some of the fish out of the hold as the hatch door is now open. The pride of the fishing fleet in Dunmore, one of the best and most talked-about boats on the south and south-east coasts, has been tossed to the bottom of the sea like a paper boat.

And then there is silence inside the boat.

All human life has been extinguished.

It is completely and utterly dark.

It is over.

*

When a tragedy occurs at sea and men are lost, their relatives are always focused on reclaiming the bodies. The need for a body, for a moment to say goodbye, is overwhelming for those left behind. Without it, they are left in a vacuum of grief, forced to accept their loved one is gone forever, but always afflicted with an irrational hope that if there wasn't a body, there wasn't a death. For the families, a recovery operation is paramount.

In March 2007 Pat Hennessy and others called for the *Pere Charles* to be lifted. Some relatives are very concerned by the attitude of the Marine Casualty Investigation Board (MCIB). They feel that without the vessel itself, the MCIB will be reduced to theorising about weather and stability in trying to determine the cause of the sinking. If there was a mechanical fault as well, which some feel is very possible, this fact cannot be ascertained without raising the vessel. As a result, the relatives predict that the MCIB report will paint broad, general brushstrokes, but will not answer the important question: what were the total elements that combined to cause the *Pere Charles* to sink?

For a number of reasons, including the fact that the *Honey Dew* is breaking up and divers have been into every section, the relatives of Ger and Tomasz have not called for that boat to be lifted.

The Marine Casualty Investigation Board argues that in all losses at sea, its brief is to find fact, not fault. It does not need to raise vessels in order to ascertain the facts.

When the 2007 General Election is called for the last week in May, the families make a brave and bold step: they decide to run candidates in constituencies such as Waterford and Wexford, and possibly even in Kerry and Cork. Within a week the government announces that the *Pere Charles* will be raised, along with the *Maggie B.* Regardless of the motive behind it, the families are delighted with the decision and in return agree not to put forward candidates.

In September 2007, contracts are awarded to an Irish diving company to raise both boats. At time of going to print, he boats are due to be lifted in October 2007: another harrowing and emotional few weeks for the relatives.

16

Lessons in Survival

'What makes the sea? A farmer knows how much he loves the land, he knows all the mysteries of growth, he walks it, he knows every turn, every sod. The guys out at sea have same feeling about their 'fields', the same love, the same hate for it as a farmer has for his land. The draw of the sea is unbelieveable. It's a magical place. It's never the same any day. I know that for fishermen it's exciting and there's a buzz about pulling up a net full of fish, of coming into port with the holds full. And then there's the disappointment of a bad day's fishing. A yachtsman will know what his risk factors are and at the end of the day, he doesn't have to win the race; but fishermen have to make a living out of the sea,

230

a yachtsman can take down the sail and go home, the fishermen can't do that. Fishermen are tough, hard men; they go out in all kinds of weather . . . I'd hate to have to do it.'[3]

Fishing is in the blood; the sea is in the blood. Fishermen usually follow a generational line of fishermen, emulating their father, grandfathers and great-grandfathers. In fishing communities, the only way to look is out to sea, the only freedom is on the waves – it infuses these people's lives as much as it provides the lifeline of economic survival. But we don't often think about our fishermen, or the hardships they face. When we go into a restaurant, we marvel at how Irish people now think nothing of paying €20–€30 for a fish main course; thinking to ourselves how the fishermen must be coining it in. It isn't true. What is true is that fishing now constitutes one of the most dangerous jobs in the world. We need to ask: why? And what can we do to make it safer?

*

As a workplace, the sea is unique in every way – in the joy it can give and in the threats it poses. You could be forgiven for thinking that fishermen are a pampered lot, recompensed highly for the risks they take everyday to land their catch. The problem is that the fishing industry is so tiny, it has absolutely no leverage in terms of political clout. Figures from the Central Statistics Office show that just 0.56 per cent of the national workforce is employed in the fishing industry. There are almost 5,000 people employed directly in fishing, while another 1,936 work in the aquaculture sector (i.e.

---

[3]Quote from a senior officer of the MCIB.

fish farming), 3,507 work in processing and 1,185 work in ancillary services in and around harbours. That's a total of 11,615 people, which means fishermen make up just 0.24 per cent of the workforce. To put it in perspective: there are more hairdressers in Ireland; there are 5,000 people working in one Intel factory in Dublin alone. And when you are that far in the minority, it can be very hard to make your voice heard.

Government figures show that from the year 2000 up to and including 2006, nineteen people have been killed in Irish waters while trying to make a living from fishing. This means that over that six-year period, a person was nearly four times more likely to die in fishing than in farming, and nearly eight times more likely to die in fishing than on a building site. In most workplace accidents, there is rarely more than one person killed at any one time. But fishing is the exception because if a boat sinks, an entire crew can be lost. And it remains one of the only professions in the world where bodies are sometimes never recovered. The tragedy of somebody dying on a building site or in a factory is bad enough, but how much worse would it be if the distraught relatives didn't have a body to bury?

Fishing remains one of the most dangerous jobs in the world, and fishermen have the highest fatal-accident rate of any type of worker in the North Atlantic countries. As Tom McSweeney, Marine Correspondent for RTÉ, notes:

> 'Fishermen get little sympathy until tragedy strikes. They work to earn a living for their families but unlike most of us, do so in more dangerous circumstances. Economic circumstances have a part in forcing fishermen to sea in what many ashore would consider bad weather.

Fishermen are locked in an economic battle to stay afloat, they want to fish, they love to fish, they are happy to earn their living this way, but they are finding that their efforts are being strangulated by unsympathetic policies and bureaucracy at its worst.'

Many fishermen feel that for years now the fishing industry has been neglected by a succession of uncaring governments, that they live in a world that neither understands their position or wishes to help them. They feel attacked on three fronts: reduced quotas, rising fuel prices and a hostile government attitude. They believe governments over the past forty years have shown a consistent disregard for fishing, with the main problem stemming back to the decision by the Fianna Fáil government (in negotiating our EEC entry in the early 1970s) to give away fishing rights in favour of more subsidies for farmers. It came down to votes; there were more farmers than fishermen.

The government's attitude is a moot point, with the officials counter-arguing the fishermen's allegations. But rising fuel prices are simply a dismal reality.

It costs Johnny Walsh, skipper of the *Rachel Jay*, €22,000 a year for insurance. Stocking the boat with food for the crew for a five-day expedition costs between €300 and €400. Then there are maintenance costs, which can vary greatly, and crew wages, which are on average at least €350 a man. The skipper has to earn his wage, too. And, finally, in order to keep all the balls in the air, the repayments have to be made on the bank loans. In total, then, it can cost a trawler skipper €8,000–€10,000 just to take his boat out fishing for a week. When you are caught in this sort of economic bind, you only have two choices: get out of the business, or upgrade to a bigger boat and work even harder and for longer hours.

When it comes to the pressures being brought to bear on fishermen, particularly from the quota system, Nicko Murphy, a fish buyer in Dunmore, believes that some civil servants are out of control:

> 'Some have never even been on board a boat and they are putting men under awful pressure to catch a quota in a specified amount of time instead of being allowed to catch the quota at their leisure. The *Pere Charles* should have been allowed to carry-over its quota for the following week instead of having to fill the boat because that was the only day they are going to get out because of the forecast. '

Fishermen have to provide for their families and when the weather is bad, they have very little chance to do that. Nicko feels the pressure to look after the bank manager is pushing fishermen into doing things they know aren't wise:

> 'Fifteen or twenty years ago the bank manager had to be looked after as well, but fishermen could go off and catch their quota at their leisure; in fact, there wasn't a quota. They could catch fish the week after, but now they're being forced out in weather they shouldn't be out in. The biggest pressure comes from the quota system and from the Department. Fishermen are trying to duck and dive and hide quotas and jig them around to try to fit the bill. And I think decommissioning is going to make it worse as it's going to be harder for exporters to fill lorries; I think the Department and the government should be looking for better quota.'

Each December the EU instructs the Department of Marine as to the total Irish quota for the forthcoming year, then it's up to Department officials to liaise with the fishery organisations to divide the quota up as best it can amongst all the boats that are fishing each month.

Fishermen cannot understand how the government can justify a regulation that doesn't allow a boat into port unless a fishery officer gives permission; that forces every boat to ring the fishery officer to give advance notice of its arrival; and that allows boats to land only at certain ports. Worst of all, when a catch exceeds the quota – whether by default or design – the extra fish must be simply discarded because there are no arrangements in place to deal with this situation. In the eyes of Ireland's fishing communities, the EU's Common Fisheries Policy has destroyed the industry here and elsewhere, which is incredible given that Ireland has the richest waters in Europe and consumer demand is higher than ever.

Many fishermen feel that when they make suggestions on how to improve matters, all they hear from the Department officials is a resounding 'No': 'No, we can't do that, Brussels wouldn't agree'. As a result, all they see is their quotas being whittled away, making it harder and harder for them to survive.

Scientists and the EU reckon that cod and many other fish are being over-fished in European waters. Many fishermen estimate they are killing twice as many fish as they are being allowed to keep. They see a possible solution in a relaxation of the rules, so that a boat might be able to bring in 5 per cent more than its allowed quota and then maybe have to tie up on the dock for an extra day at the end of the month because of this: at least it would mean less fish being dumped at sea.

Exacerbating the problems posed by the quota is the fact that Irish fishermen face stiff competition from international vessels, which is where the legal waters can get very muddied indeed. The Spaniards have always had a very strong fisheries lobby, with ministers who bang the table a lot in European Commission meetings. As far as Tom McSweeney of RTÉ is concerned, they have basically raped Irish waters because there is very little fish left off the coast of Spain:

> 'The Irish government got very narked when figures came out showing that countries such as Spain, Portugal, France, and Holland have over the years taken out of Irish waters fish the value of which exceeds *all* of the grants given by the EU to Ireland. *All the grants combined!* The value of fish is massive. A lot of the big Spanish boats land in Castletown-bere; the fish go straight into lorries and off to Spain.'

Many Irish fishermen believe the Irish authorities are 'soft' on Spanish and French boats, and that they get away with a lot more than the Irish lads do. The government denies this.

Of course, the Spanish and French boats are also under fierce pressure; many Spanish fish companies have closed down and many French boats have been sold off. Many Irish fishermen say Spanish and French boats regularly land fish when there is no fishery officer there to check their catch. But the fact is a fishery officer will not be checking every box that comes off a trawler, no matter if it is Irish, Spanish, or French. Other fishermen believe that no log sheet tells the whole truth as everybody has to cheat a little, that no one could survive in the business otherwise. A fisherman who, for example, puts down on a log-book that he has five boxes of conger eels is obviously not telling the truth.

For all the arguing, fishing can't happen if there are no fish in the water. The latest figures suggest that 75 per cent of fish stocks in the waters around Ireland are being harvested beyond their safe biological limits. It is also estimated that half of all fish stocks across the world are fully exploited, and another one-quarter are over-exploited or depleted. In 2004, 700,000 tonnes of fish were taken out of Irish waters, most of it by Spanish and French boats; over the last decade, Irish fishermen have caught 250,000 tonnes per year.

Irish boats are allowed to catch two-thirds of the cod caught in the Irish 200-mile zone, but stocks are decreasing (the spawning stock in the Irish Sea for cod is estimated to have fallen from 21,000 tonnes in 1973 to only 5,000 tonnes in 2006). This has meant that the amount of cod landed by Irish boats has fallen 78 per cent between 1995 and 2004 (whiting and haddock are also down massively). So for 2006, 11,867 tonnes of cod, whiting and haddock were allowed to be caught by Irish boats, with an overall value of €12 million. Irish fishermen were also allowed to catch 35,334 tonnes of herring, with a total value of €5 million.

The EU's top administrators believe quota systems, net restrictions and limits on how many boats can fish in any one area are the best way of ensuring that there will still be fish in EU waters in twenty years time. One of the main prongs in the defence of fishing stocks is to decommission boats and thereby reduce the number of boats fishing the waters. The Irish government has adopted and implemented this policy over the past few years.

At the moment there are 1,844 boats licensed as part of the Irish fishing fleet. The average age of the boats is twenty-four years. In the past decade, seventy-nine new and more modern second-hand boats have entered the fleet; 300 older vessels have left; thirty-five boats were 'decommissioned' between 2000 and 2006 at a cost of €14 million (an average of €400,000 per boat); and 180 onboard jobs were lost.

Government officials get annoyed when fishermen and reporters accuse them of not understanding the problems faced by fishermen. Officials know they are not fishermen, but they believe it's their job to work with fishermen, to listen to scientists, to understand the needs of fishing communities, to learn how and why the complexities of Brussels work, and to try to ensure there is a fishing industry in Ireland in twenty years time, not just next year. They say they know how hard it is for fishermen and they realise why fishermen sometimes vent their anger on the government. They know fishermen don't like the Common Fisheries Policy because it is restrictive and because anything that stops fishermen from taking more fish out of the sea is something they will naturally rail against.

The government argues that fishing has changed radically from a time when there was a belief that the sea could continuously yield up fish forever. In the past, if you over-fished a particular stock, you moved onto another type and came back a few years later and it would be back to old levels. That's simply not the case in our modern world. The most dramatic such example of the consequences of over-fishing in recent decades was the wiping out of the cod stocks off Newfoundland in Canada, which left up to 900 communities devastated.

As with so many of our older trades, this is the crux of the matter: how our old, once self-sustaining industries can compete in the modern age, without disrupting the environment unduly. But while we must respect the notion of collective responsibility and conservation for the future, it is also necessary to assess the reality on the ground and to understand that legislating for the global can pose very serious risks – both economic and physical – to the individual.

*

So, then, if we are talking about improving the lot of fishermen, what practical steps can be taken to achieve this? While the area of policy is contentious and both sides will argue their points vociferously, in the area of safety at sea, the problems and solutions are a little more clear-cut.

One simple change could immediately improve safety at sea: the government should abolish VAT on lifejackets and safety equipment. At present, the VAT on these items is 21 per cent; that is disgraceful.

The government could also give more support to fishermen who want to train and retrain. Any person who is skippering a boat greater than 17m in length is supposed to have a 'Skipper's Certificate'. To be blunt about it, they need to pay fishermen to do the courses. At present, Bord Iascaigh Mhara (BIM) provides skipper's courses in Castletownbere in Co. Cork and Greencastle in Co. Donegal. The basic course takes fourteen weeks, and those who have done it say that it was hugely beneficial. The problem is that many fishermen put off not doing it for another day because they simply cannot afford to be away for three-and-a-half months and not earning a wage. Who could? Tom Hennessy didn't have a Skipper's Certificate but it didn't make him a lesser skipper. He had years of experience both on deck and in the wheelhouse and was considered a very able and competent skipper. How could he have gone to Castletownbere every week for fourteen weeks and not have money coming in to support Lulu and his two daughters?

And some of the best skippers in the country don't have Skipper's Certificates. Plus, there is nothing to suggest that if Tom had done a skipper's course, the outcome on that fateful Wednesday evening of 10 January would have been different. It's one of those devilish catch-22 situations.

There are still many fishermen who don't know how to swim. Traditionally, they have had the attitude: 'if I'm going overboard and I'm going to die, there's no point in fighting it; the sea takes its own, why struggle?' It is an attitude that was adopted by many *currach* fishermen on the islands off the west coast of Ireland. However, BIM centres are finding that a lot of older fishermen are coming back to learn how to swim and how to use a lifejacket. The instructors feel it would also be beneficial to train fishermen in the stability of boats, which is probably the most important aspect of any vessel. Again, these courses need to be set up and funded, and the fishermen need to be given incentives to undertake them.

One simple safety measure would be to provide each fisherman with a hand-held, waterproof VHF, or personalised EPIRB, small enough to be attached to a lifejacket. If a man goes overboard, either device would be able to transmit a far-reaching Mayday signal. These should be provided free of charge to each fisherman

The main safety concern for many officials within the Department of the Marine is the lack of construction and stability regulations with boats in the 15–24m (49–78ft) bracket. Since 2004, there has been a very strong Code of Practice for boats less than 15m (49ft) in length, and there are tough regulations for boats over 24m (78ft) . Amazingly, in the 15–24m range there are very few regulations regarding stability tests for boats that have had modifications. In total, 61 per cent of all lives lost on fishing boats in Irish waters from 1996 to 2006 were caused by stability problems. This is another area where subsidies could be put to good use. For a trawler to undergo stability tests, it means weeks of surveys – time fishermen can ill-afford to lose. But the increasing numbers of fatalities suggest it is high time such tests became the norm in the industry. It will take government support to make this come to pass.

The frontline of the government's defence of our fishermen is the Marine Survey Office, based in Dublin. This is the great white hope for improving standards in the industry, but it has an uphill slog all the way. Brian Hogan is Chief Surveyor and has a team of surveyors around the country, who check the construction, stability and buoyancy of boats in the Irish fishing fleet.

There are essentially no rules for the 300 or so vessels in the group of 15–24m fishing vessels when modifications are made that may affect stability, and for a long time Brian Hogan has been saying that it's within this group that most boats are sinking.

Officials have been calling on the government for years to implement new regulations to ensure all sectors of the fleet are covered. Some officials believe the reason they haven't been brought in to cover the 15–24m sector is because of the impact it would have on the fishing industry. The majority of the country's fishing trawlers fall into this sector, and if tomorrow the government was to test the stability of each and every one, it could cripple the industry. It would mean taking each boat out of service for weeks; the cost to each skipper and fishing boat-owner would be astronomical. The only solution is to phase in the tests over a five-year period and to compensate boat-owners for time lost at sea. To achieve this, the Marine Survey Office would also have to be provided with a larger budget to hire more staff.

As long as the Survey Office is under-staffed, the general perception will be that safety at sea is not a priority for the government. Safety legislation cannot be enforced if there are not enough staff to carry out audits. Furthermore, we still have no national safety plan in place and no State salvage facility.

Marine surveyors believe that if you want to stop accidents, surveyors are the people for the job. Surveyors argue that if the government grant-aided stability tests, every €1 spent here would save €1,000 being spent on 'end of line' solutions, such as rescue services. While lifeboats and SAR will always be needed, more emphasis should be placed on stability tests. In September 2007, the government announced it is to introduce new regulations for trawlers 15-24m in length.

*

It is clear that the problems and challenges facing the fishing industry and individual fishermen are numerous. The sinking of the *Pere Charles* and the *Honey Dew*, the loss of seven men, these are events that should shake us to the core and make us resolve to find the solutions and implement them, regardless of the difficulties inherent in doing so. We have a fine tradition of fishing in this country and some of the richest fishing waters in the world, that is worth fighting for. It's worth protecting.

Epilogue

In the months that follow the tragedy, five-year-old Christine talks a lot about her Dad. She says that if she dies, she wants to be with Mummy, 'because I don't want to miss you as much as I missed my daddy.'

She often draws a picture, or writes a letter, which she leaves under her pillow for her Dad. She likes him to see how good she's getting at her drawing and writing. When she wakes in the morning, it's gone.

*

A sunny wind blows across the sand dunes and horses munch on the commonage of the Magharees in Co. Kerry. Mount Brandon and Slieve Mish lean away. Electricity poles tilt, up to their ankles in water. The wilted signs for the surf school having survived another winter. Tom Hennessy's father, known as Tom Apple, is down at the small pier from where he used to fish and to where he always returned. But now one of his sons will never return.

On this peninsula, every place has meaning and memories: Fitzgerald's in Castlegregory, a bar/hostel/shop/off-licence, a place to take stock on a Sunday before dinner; the graveyard, where, before the diving, Tom Apple and Julia had made preparations for the return of their son's body; the couch in the family home where at Christmas Pat Frank and Tom spoke about how lucky Tom was with Lulu and two lovely children and things going so well; their son's smiling face on the worn-out DVD of Tony's wedding in September 2006.

On the window-sill beside the open window, a card is battling not to be blown over by a gust of wind. It's a card sent by a friend to remember a friend, Tom:

> *Just as the mist it rises and vanishes out to sea,*
> *Tom too has come and left you today.*
> *It seems like a dream that he was so much part of your*
> *   lives,*
> *That he lived and loved as you do.*
> *Now he has left your hearts and his home like the fish that*
> *   the fishermen threw back into the sea to go on its way.*
> *And that is what Tom is doing today,*
> *To a bright new world.*
> *See the sun glitter as he drifts from sight,*
> *Though your tears are bitter, you know that he, like the*
> *   salmon leaps,*
> *Will always be there in your memories deep.*

And below: 'When you are facing in the right direction, all you have to do is keep walking.'

Near the family home is a games room, which Tom's younger brother Dan furnished with a pool table and chairs. On the wall, a small prayer, put there by Tom last year. Not the type of thing he'd normally do, but for some reason, he did. It reads:

A little more kindness,
A little less greed,
A little more giving,
A little less creed.

A little more smile,
A little less frown,
A little less kicking
A man when he's down.

A little more "we",
A little less "I",
A little more laugh,
A little less cry.

A little more flowers,
More for life,
Fewer on graves,
At the end of the strife.

And back in the house, Pat Frank tries to find solace in words, in a poem he has written:

I'm dreaming of my two fine boys who from Kilshanney
came,
They disappeared one winter's night ten days into the year,
They left no mark on land or shore for the sea was their
domain,
And that they did mention their minds and part of it they
became.
Their stories were all fishy tales, their songs of boat and
sail,
Just as reality lives on land and sea, legend prevails.

> They care not that no earthly stone will mark their resting
>   place,
> For into legend they have done and forever there will sail.

The events of that week affected people all round the country, even those areas far from the sea. The children of third and fourth class in Loughmore National School near Templemore, in Co. Tipperary wrote poems and drew pictures in an attempt to understand what they were feeling. Instigated by their teacher Mary O'Brien under the theme of 'water safety', they got information from the RNLI, watched water safety videos, watched news reports on television, got a visit from a lifeguard and also went to watch the two-actor play 'Lifeboat' which was on nationwide tour at the time. The pupils wrote of their sadness for the families, and especially for the children left behind.

The relatives of the seven men have all received massive support from communities in Ireland and abroad, for which they are very grateful. Some of the messages written to the Hennessy family read:

> 'Words are so inadequate and cannot express this properly but I think you know the great regard we always had for Tomaisín and Pat and now life goes on without them. But Tomaisín lives on in his beautiful daughters. I met them and their mother in the Green Room at New Year and thought what a lovely family they were. None of us knows where the strength comes from to keep on going but it does come and we are able to face the future no matter how hard it is . . . so with deep sympathy and much love . . .'

> 'For a parent to have a child go before them is very hard to

bear. To lose both a son and a brother at the same time is unimaginable.'

'The first night when it came on the radio I thought it was my son when they said a skipper from Kerry living in Dunmore East . . . I have prayed every day and night since, hoping that they will all be got . . . the weather has been cruel to us all.'

'What is dying? A ship sails and I stand watching till she fades on the horizon, and someone at my side says, "She is gone". Gone where? Gone from my sight, that is all; she is just as large as when I saw her . . . The diminished size and total loss of sight is in me, not in her, and just at the moment when someone at my side says "she is gone", there are others who are watching her coming, and other voices take up a glad shout, "there she comes!" . . . and that is dying."
(A printed message from Bishop Brent.)

'Words cannot express the deep sorrow we feel for you; Tomaisín and Pat were taken from you during the performance of their duty   such a precarious profession was theirs. January 2007 will forever be a landmark never forgotten.'

Aine Uí Fhoghlú, a poet and songwriter from Ring in Co. Waterford, sees a newspaper picture of Mary Bohan standing on the quay in Kinsale, looking out to sea; it inspires her to write 'Come Dance with Me Fisherman':

She stands on the pier barely holding back the tears
Remembering the final words he spoke
Staring at the ocean wide as winter kills the fading light
Her fading heart still dares to harbour hope
Tonight she'll count the stars out from her bedroom window
And she'll try to believe he's coming home
Try to picture him a while as he said that last goodbye
She saw the ocean dancing in his eyes

Chorus:
Come dance with me fisherman, dance in my dreams
I'll put on my best dress and loosen my hair
Your brave arms around me, your warmth it surrounds me
Sea breezes singing our song on the air

For Mary, and all those who are grieving, the support from the communities has been steadfast and generous, but their grief is never-ending. Mary cries many nights for her devoted husband Ger. Her sobs are silent, so that her children can't hear her.

*

The summer sun glints on the Memorial Wall in Dunmore. Tourists stop to read the lines inscribed from a poem written by John O'Connor. He wrote the words in the 1970s as lyrics to a song, a song that has never been sung. They were inspired by a story told by his father, who was a fisherman, whose own father was lost at sea and his body never recovered. His name is one of the many on the wall.

On misty nights off Dunmore East, so the story goes,
Twinkling lights far out at sea shine out in sad repose,

No one knows who they are, but the talk is on the quays,
They're the ghosts of long lost ships and men who sailed the
 seas.

Spanish galleons, fishing smacks, a German submarine,
Lie together 'neath the waves where light is never seen,
But, perhaps, a teardrop finds its way to the moonlight up
 above,
The light reflected sends a sign to the ones one shore they
 love.

Say a prayer for the souls of the sea who'll never reach the
 land,
They say as many men lie there as there are grains of sand,
They'll haul their nets, hoist their sails, set their course no
 more,
Say a prayer for the souls of the sea, who rest just off
 Dunmore.

Thus concludes 'The Souls of the Sea'.

Acknowledgements

I would like to thank all those who have helped in what, for many, were very emotional and difficult times. Especially to the families and friends of those who have died; this book would not have been possible without your help and cooperation and was written so that the memory of the seven who died will not be forgotten; your courage in the face of awful tragedy and loss is inspiring beyond words.

I would also like to thank also those who agreed to be interviewed, both on the record and off the record; without you, this publication would not have been possible.

I would like to thank Denis Harding, Michael Walsh, Johnny Walsh, Ebby Sheehan, Brendan O'Driscoll, Nicko Murphy, Joefy Murphy, Brian Murphy, Marco Power and those dozens of other fishermen in Castletownbere, Kinsale, Dunmore East, Passage East, Kilmore Quay and along the south and south east coast who spoke with me in the belief that a book such as this is important for those in coastal communities.

And to those fishermen from abroad who have come and have to come to Ireland in an attempt to earn a living.

I would also like to thank all those involved in the Irish Coast Guard: Jim Griffin, Joan Bowe, Martina McCarthy, Chris Reynolds, Dave McMeyler, Ger Hegarty, Norman Fullam, Geoff Livingstone; and Seamus Power; and all those hundreds who volunteered during January and February 2007 and continue to offer their services when the need arises. I would also like to thank those in the Irish Navy for their help – Eugene Ryan, Terry Ward, Darragh Kirwan, Tony O'Regan and all those in the diving section of the Navy; your courage and skill is admirable and a great service to everyone. And for the same reason, thanks also to Sgt. John Connolly and Sgt. John Bruton and all those in the Garda Underwater Unit.

A special thanks to those brave men and women involved in helicopter Search and Rescue around the coast, especially Dara Fitzpatrick, Barry O'Connor, Paul Truss, Neill McAdam, and all those based at Waterford Regional Airport SAR.

To those in the RNLI, especially Neville Murphy, Joefy Murphy, Peter Curran, Paul Tuohy, Ray Power, Michael Hurley: all the RNLI volunteers around the country are heroes through and through.

Individuals who also deserve much thanks include Paddy Mason, John Walsh, Kathleen Power, Sandra Mason White, John White, my parents Sean and Ann Tiernan, my brother Ronan and sisters Michelle, Karen and Anita, Stephen Bance, Margaret Kenny, Rosaline Kelly, Inga Grubinskaite, Angus Ritchie, Brian Hogan, Dylan Vaughan, Michael Williams in NUIG, Johnny O'Connor, Michael Bance, Peter Gillick, Peter O'Brien, Margaret Cott, Kathleen Power, Eamonn O'Neill, Helen Cummins, Lorcan O'Cinneide, Willemine Phelan and all at Met Eireann, John Leech, Badiul Alam and all at the National Maritime College,

Martyn Simpson, Tony McLoughlin, Phil Davitt, Brian Nolan, Michael Parsons, Sarah Murphy, Neans McSweeney, Paul Byrne, Barry Roche, Ralph Reigel, Tom McSweeney, Lorna Siggins, Ann Mooney, the CSO in Cork, Aine ni Fhoghlu, Ken Cleary, Johnny Clunno, Veronica Scanlon, Nick Carecn in Newfoundland, Garda Superintendent Tom Saunderson, and those in the MCIB and Dept of Marine with whom I spoke privately. And anybody I forgot to mention. And a special, special thanks to Peter and Trudy Francis for their years of friendship and to Peter's superb dedication and work on this project throughout 2007.

To my editors Ciara Considine and Claire Rourke and all at HHI – thank you for putting your trust in me. To all those in RTÉ, including Helen McInerney, Ciaran Mullooly, Donal Wylde, Neilus Dennehy, Brian Walsh, Conan Doyle, Melanie Kehoe, Justine O'Mahony, Tom McSweeney, Conor Mark Kavanagh, Jim Wylde, Jacqui Corcoran, Ed Mulhall, Cillian de Paor, Ray Burke, Conor Fennell and Donal Byrne.

And, most especially, to my wife Louise and our two fabulous children, Isobel (5) and Sam (2). Without you Louise, this book would not have been possible; thank you for all your support, help and love. And for Isobel and Sam, this book is about dolphins, sea horses, star fishes and of course, mermaids.

*

The publisher would like to thank the following for kind permission to reproduce images and lyrics:

Photos: The Bohan, Coady, Dyrin, Hennessy and Jagly families; Brian Cleare; Steve Humphries/Independent Newspapers; Donal Wylde/RTÉ news; Patrick Browne Photography, New Ross; Provision, Cork; The Irish Coast Guard; *The Marine Times*.

Lyrics: Johnny O'Connor, Roc Music, Avondale, Waterford City, for 'Souls of the Sea'; Aine Uí Fhoghlú for 'Come Dance with Me Fisherman'.